IDENTITY
LEADERSHIP

IDENTITY
LEADERSHIP

*To Lead Others You Must First
Lead Yourself*

STEDMAN
GRAHAM

**CENTER
STREET**

New York Nashville

Center Street
Hachette Book Group
1290 Avenue of the Americas, New York, NY 10104
centerstreet.com
twitter.com/centerstreet

First Edition: May 2019

Center Street is a division of Hachette Book Group, Inc. The Center Street name and logo are trademarks of Hachette Book Group, Inc.

The publisher is not responsible for websites (or their content) that are not owned by the publisher.

The Hachette Speakers Bureau provides a wide range of authors for speaking events. To find out more, go to www.HachetteSpeakersBureau.com or call (866) 376-6591.

Library of Congress Cataloging-in-Publication Data has been applied for.

ISBNs: 978-1-5460-8337-5 (hardcover), 978-1-5460-8336-8 (ebook)

Printed in the United States of America

LSC-C

10 9 8 7 6 5 4 3 2 1

To my brother, James Graham, a special man for whom
I care deeply and from whom I've learned so much.

Contents

Introduction

Identity leadership is very important to me. It's a topic that is relevant to the 7.7 billion people living today. Identity leadership is self-leadership, and it is based on the philosophy that if you can't lead yourself, you can't lead anyone else.

Leadership, or lack thereof, determines the success or failure of an organization. Identity, the true understanding of self, can serve as a leader's greatest asset. Enduringly successful people know who they are, are clear about what matters to them, and create value for themselves and others.

Identity leadership holds you responsible for your own development. Identity leaders never stop growing or developing. They are lifelong students and never stop taking in new information.

My life dramatically changed for the better when I began centering all that I do around my talents, strengths, and passions. As I came to understand my identity and my purpose in life, that enabled me to realize the value of education, information, and knowledge. I began to make information relevant to my personal and professional development, and that allowed me to define my existence and take control of my life. The old system of memorizing information to take a test and then forgetting the information makes it difficult to grow beyond our circumstances.

Understanding how to apply knowledge and learning to self-actualize your potential is what identity leadership is all about. The

Nine-Step Success Process, which I present in this book, works. It will help you reverse the old and ineffective learning process and make everything relevant to who you are.

We all have twenty-four hours in a day. The question is, what do we do with those twenty-four hours to empower ourselves? What are we doing to develop our gifts, our strengths, our talents?

My goal with this book is to improve your performance at every level, enhance your lifelong learning capacity, and change your mindset from that of a follower to a leader—first leading yourself, then others. I've dedicated my life to this work of teaching people throughout the world how to self-actualize their potential as human beings. I am thankful and blessed to have discovered for myself who I am and what my purpose is, what my mission in life is, and to be able to share that with as many people as I possibly can.

If you want your life to get better, then take control of it. It's up to you and no one else. Don't wait for others to define who you are or what your potential is. That, my friend, is a lifelong journey for you to undertake.

Stedman Graham
Chicago, Illinois

IDENTITY
LEADERSHIP

CHAPTER 1

The Call for Identity Leaders

*Identity development changes your thinking about
what is possible.*

Carrie Ponder had a lofty vision for a single mother of eight living in inner-city Chicago: she wanted all of her children to reach their full potential and flourish in their chosen fields. Many in her position would not dare dream of such happiness and fulfillment; they would assume it was unattainable.

But Carrie Ponder held fast to her vision, and she ordered her day by it. What fell in line with that vision, she did; what did not feed or nourish that vision, she did not do.

She enrolled her children in youth centers, church organizations, and library programs.[1] She found affordable weekend tickets to plays, museums, and the opera. She turned even mundane city-wide bus rides into the remarkable, pointing out the various architecture along the way and engaging her children in conversation about it.

For ten years, Carrie Ponder and her eight children lived in a three-bedroom apartment. They moved to another apartment building, and it burned to the ground a week later. They lost most of their possessions in that fire.

Carrie Ponder did not let life or that fire defeat her or her children. The fire had taken their material goods, but it had not taken their minds or their spirits or their vision or their potential. She taught her children that their pockets might be empty, but their minds and spirits were rich and full.

Carrie Ponder sent her children to Princeton, to the University of Chicago, to Northwestern University, and to the University of Pennsylvania. She raised a lawyer, an advertising executive, a teacher, and a doctoral student.

She raised her children in such a way that they fulfilled her vision: they reached their full potential and are flourishing in their fields.

Carrie Ponder knew who she was. She knew who her children were. She did not let life's circumstances define her or her kids. Instead, she opened the door for them to fulfilling, enriching lives.

That is understanding your true identity and demonstrating strong leadership combined.

Carrie Ponder epitomizes identity leadership.

The point is not to become a leader. The point is to become yourself.

—WARREN BENNIS

DEFINING IDENTITY LEADERSHIP

For more than thirty years, I have been writing books, teaching in colleges, working in communities, leading nonprofits, and speaking and conducting workshops around the world. In all that time, I have come to know one thing: leadership is everything.

The needs of the twenty-first century cannot be met by followers. The opportunities opening up in the twenty-first century will not be snatched up by followers. The world will not be improved by followers.

It is leaders who will meet those needs, seize those opportunities, and change the world.

Identity leadership is the highest order of leadership. It is a different kind of leadership that is required in the twenty-first century—found in people who are aware of their own intentions and identity, who responsibly lead themselves to overcome obstacles in their own lives and, as a result, lead others to succeed in driving organizational growth.

Without a strong identity, we are more likely to be carried by the influence of our environment into a future requiring very little reflection or development. I have spent my career helping organizations address the leadership gap at every level, because filling that gap is critical to the success of the organization. But to close that gap, we have to understand the nature of true leadership. True leaders are not looking to posture; true leaders are looking to make a difference and to fulfill their mission in life and business.

Identity leadership is the highest order of leadership. It is a different kind of leadership that is required in the twenty-first century.

Linking Identity with Leadership

For most of my career, I have helped people explore and understand their identity, guiding them through the process of clarifying their passions, purpose, and plans to align their visions for their lives with their realities.

Now I am taking that a step further, linking identity to the concept of leadership. These two concepts, when brought into sync with each other, meld into a powerful entity that transforms people's lives.

That's what this entire book and my identity leadership program are about: transforming your life, opening doors to potential and to opportunities that you didn't even know existed.

I am helping you become an identity leader, something I believe the world sorely needs.

So, what is an identity leader?

Definition of an Identity Leader

Identity leaders know themselves inside and out.

They are at peace with who they are.

They don't make excuses for not being strong in every area or for not being perfect. They know their strengths, and they see how to use their strengths to their own and to an organization's benefit.

They know what they care about and what they are passionate about, and they pour their energies into these passions.

They know how to build teams and be part of a team.

They know how to lead, how to encourage, how to motivate others—and themselves.

They are authentic leaders who lead others with the skills they've developed.

They do not give up.

They stand strong on their principles.

They aren't ruled by fear or other negative emotions.

They are problem solvers.

They see solutions where others see only roadblocks.

They are bridge builders and people connectors.

They see the potential not only in themselves but in others, and they nurture that potential. They bring an energy and unflagging enthusiasm to their work.

They fully expect to fail and to learn from that failure and to be better because of it.

They look forward to each day because of the possibilities it holds.

They naturally attract others because of their vitality, their optimism, and the value they bring to any group they are in.

They remain unfazed by the difficulties of life.

They know who they are, they know where they are going, and they know how they are going to get there. And because they know these things, people follow them and respect them. People pay attention to those who have a vision and who know how to live that vision out, step by step, day by day, decision by decision.

THE NEED FOR IDENTITY LEADERSHIP IN A CHANGING WORLD

If there is one constant in the world, it is change. Here are just a few recent examples of the seismic changes in various industries brought about by disruptive innovation—which happens when a company introduces an innovation that disrupts an existing market and creates a new market, displacing established market-leading firms and products:

- Throughout the 1990s, Blockbuster was the dominant firm in the video rental market. By 2004, it employed over 80,000 people and had more than 9,000 stores worldwide. By 2010, it had filed for bankruptcy. What happened? Netflix, a startup in the industry, grew to dominance with a new delivery system and business model. Ironically, Blockbuster turned down multiple opportunities to buy Netflix for just $50 million in 2000. In 2017, Netflix had total assets of over $19 billion.
- When Amazon came on the scene in 1995, Borders bookstore was generating about $1.6 billion a year in sales. The company employed about 19,500 people in more than 600 stores throughout the US. In 2011, Borders filed for bankruptcy. The consensus

was that Borders was too late to the web (Borders' online sales redirected to Amazon, which hurt Borders' branding), it was too late to e-books, it had too many stores, and it was offering a glut of books when people were shifting to online purchasing. Borders had too much debt, and it over-invested in music sales, getting into CD sales just about the time that music file sharing was becoming popular. As for Amazon, they are the largest internet company in the world, with a revenue of $232 billion in 2018.

- Uber is the biggest automobile transportation company in the world—with no overhead for cars. Instead, the peer-to-peer ridesharing company, founded in 2009 and worth $72 billion, uses software to attract customers. At the beginning of 2017, Uber's share of the US ride-hailing market was 84 percent.

We Live in an Ever-Changing World

Behind each of those disruptive innovations were people with great ideas who were not afraid to buck the industry standards. Those moves not only changed the lives of countless employees and customers of those innovative companies; it opened up new markets, spurred creative thinking and moves in other industries, and placed a high premium on the type of visionary leaders who can not only handle the changes that come their way but create change by going where no company has gone before.

Change is also, of course, rampant in every industry and in people's professional and personal lives through advances in technology. Here is just a smattering of examples of changes that have happened or are likely to happen in the near future, brought about by technology:

- Watson, a question-answering computer system developed by IBM, has deep and far-reaching applications in healthcare, business, education, and many other sectors.

- 3D printing has revolutionized what we create and how we create it. In China, a five-story office building was constructed through 3D printing. The same company that constructed that building also built ten houses in twenty-four hours through 3D printing. All major shoe companies have begun 3D printing shoes.
- Doctors in China gave a boy a 3D-printed spine implant in 2014. In the future, patients will not have to wait for organ transplants; hospitals will be able to bioprint them.
- In that same future, people won't own cars. They will call a driverless car with their smartphone, it will show up and drive them to their destination, and they will pay for the distance driven.
- In less than ten years, computer processors are expected to reach the processing power of the human brain. According to two Oxford researchers, about half of American jobs are at high risk of automation.

I could go on and on, but the point is clear: the world is changing, and it is changing fast. And the rate of that transformation, fueled by technology, will become ever faster.

What does that have to do with identity leadership?

Everything.

It's the identity leaders who are ushering in these changes and who are adapting the quickest to them. It's the identity leaders who can take fuller advantage of the new opportunities that are proliferating through the disruptive thinking taking place in industries and the wholesale changes that are occurring in essentially every sector around the globe. It's the identity leaders who, indeed, are changing the way we live.

Everything you want is on the other side of fear.

—JACK CANFIELD

Identity Leaders Are Not Afraid of Change

Many people resist change. It makes them feel uneasy, and it takes them out of their comfort zone. They worry and fret about what the change might bring them and how it might affect them. They fear losing the benefits of the old ways of doing business or living life, even if the change promises to bring something better.

Identity leaders are not afraid of change. In fact, they welcome it—and indeed are always assessing why change is needed, when it is right to change, and how to best bring about that change.

Sometimes it is change that helps identity leaders emerge and be recognized. Because even as the world is changing, they, at their core—their true selves, their passions, their abilities, their approach to life—don't change. Identity leaders assess the change taking place around them and adapt, seeing how they fit into that change—indeed, how they can lead that change. They see their roles in that change and step into those roles.

Tasks, roles, and environments will change. Cultures, organizations, and circumstances will change. But the essence of an identity leader does not change.

That's an identity leader in a nutshell.

Know this: you can be an identity leader. You can be that person I just described. As you continue through this book, you'll be presented with the content, ideas, and process that can help you sharpen your identity leader skills and step more fully into your potential.

Identity leaders are not afraid of change. In fact, they welcome it—and indeed are always assessing why change is needed, when it is right to change, and how to best bring about that change.

IDENTITY LEADERSHIP IS SELF-LEADERSHIP

At the beginning of this book, I talked about Carrie Ponder and how she exemplified identity leadership as she made a way out of poverty for her children to excel in professional fields. In order for her to pave the way for her children, in order for her to lead them out of poverty and into a realm where they could live out their full potential, she had to lead herself first.

Self-leadership is a most critical aspect of identity leadership. Simply put, if you want to lead others, you have to learn how to lead yourself first.

I say that to people, and oftentimes I get a quizzical look in return. I can see the question in their eyes: "Lead myself? Isn't that an automatic thing that just happens? What does that even mean?"

I know many gifted people who are called to be leaders. They have the requisite skills to lead. They have the desire and motivation, the vision and experience, and many other attributes that leaders possess. Yet, they often find themselves stalled out in their calling to be a leader. They can't figure out what's holding them back. They pour even more of their energies into learning about leadership and into the people they are charged with leading. Their focus is outward, external, on directing and managing others.

But their leadership experience is frustrating for them and for those they lead. It's a two steps forward, one step back experience—or, on some days, it's one step forward, two steps back. What's missing? Well, in their haste to rise in leadership, they have skipped over the cornerstone element: self-leadership.

Self-leadership is a most critical aspect of identity leadership. Simply put, if you want to lead others, you have to learn how to lead yourself first.

The Power of Self-Awareness

Green Peak Partners and Cornell University examined seventy-two executives at public and private companies with revenues from $50 million to $5 billion.[2] They found that the strongest predictor of overall success was high self-awareness. Those who have high self-awareness have the foundation for:

- Enhancing their performance
- Clarifying their purpose and direction
- Overcoming labels (race, gender, circumstance)
- Growing and learning
- Developing leadership skills
- Honing emotional intelligence

Every self-leader is self-aware. Are you self-aware?

DEFINING SELF-LEADERSHIP

Self-leadership, at its core, is understanding who you are.

It's understanding your abilities and your passions and your goals.

Self-leaders know where they are going and how they are going to get there.

They live and think and act intentionally.

They know what they are responsible for.

They know themselves inside and out.

They are authentic and mindful.

They are always developing their self-awareness, self-confidence, and self-efficacy.

Their self-confidence comes from their deep understanding of themselves.

Their self-efficacy—the belief that they can handle whatever comes their way—helps them to calmly assess situations, receive feedback without being sensitive to correction, and adjust to best handle challenges.

Self-leaders are disruptive thinkers, and they are not afraid to rock the boat or follow their creative and innovative thinking.

FOUR ASPECTS OF SELF-LEADERSHIP

John Ng is chief passionary officer of Meta Consulting, which provides consulting services to top international corporations. Ng, in writing about self-leadership, says there are four aspects to self-leadership:[3]

1. **Self-awareness.** You are self-aware when you are conscious of and understand your own values, perspectives, strengths, weaknesses, leadership propensities, and emotional needs.
2. **Self-management.** When you can nurture and harness your passions, abilities, emotions, and leadership capacities in your decision-making, you are a self-manager.
3. **Other-awareness.** You have other-awareness when you can acknowledge and recognize the passions, gifts, strengths, weaknesses, potential, and needs of others.
4. **Other-management.** When you can grow and motivate other people to develop their potential and fulfill the organization's objects, you are an other-manager.

Those four aspects of self-leadership are placed in that order for a reason. You have to be self-aware before you can learn how to be a self-manager and nurture your abilities, emotions, and leadership capacities. And you need both self-awareness and self-management before you can be aware of others' needs and potential. And you need that other-awareness before you can grow the potential in others.

It's also important to understand that those four aspects remain active and dynamic. It's not like passing a baton from one relay leg to the next, and then that first relay leg is finished and resting on the sidelines. It's like that first torch is lighting the next torch, and so on, and soon all four torches are lit. All are active; all are interacting with one another. Those torches don't burn out; they just collectively burn brighter.

A person who never made a mistake never tried anything new.
—ALBERT EINSTEIN

THE IMPORTANCE OF SELF-LEADERSHIP

Many successful individuals and corporations understand the importance of self-leadership. For example, Christopher Avery, CEO of Partnerwerks, Inc., and a popular presenter on agile leadership, says that "Today's workers respond to leaders who are authentic, real, principled, responsible, inspired, and courageous. Those are qualities of self-leadership. Leading yourself is 95 percent of leading others."[4] He recommends that those who want to lead first develop and believe in themselves and then find opportunities to add value that inspires them.

WHAT SELF-LEADERSHIP CAN DO FOR YOU

Self-leadership can do many things for you, but I want to point out just a few here:

- **Self-leadership transforms the way you see others.** When you appreciate your own strengths and weaknesses, your own aspirations and potential, you can do likewise with others.

- **Self-leadership helps you achieve your potential.** Self-leaders have a longevity that other leaders don't, because they tend to have higher emotional intelligence than others. Studies comparing those who thrive in leadership roles with those who barely survive indicate that emotional intelligence—rather than cognitive abilities—was a key factor.
- **Self-leadership keeps you focused on what's important.** Because you have greater self-awareness and self-presence, or sense of self, you are not swayed to sacrifice long-term results for immediate, but likely fleeting, gain.
- **Self-leadership helps you to leave the legacy you were meant to leave.** Self-leaders are the ones who rise up to make their mark, who leave a positive impact on people and organizations, who endure through good times and bad because they are grounded in who they are and in how to lead.

WHAT SELF-LEADERSHIP CAN DO FOR A COMPANY

Ken Blanchard, a management consultant and author of more than sixty books, including *The One Minute Manager*, says that four things happen when a company develops self-leaders:[5]

- **The company witnesses accelerated development** as self-leaders take control of their own development.
- **The company sees higher performance** from its self-leaders, who are more engaged and committed to the organization.
- **The company reaps the benefits of self-leaders who hold themselves accountable** to achieving their goals and executing the company's initiatives.

- **The company experiences increased innovation** as self-leaders develop creative, forward-thinking solutions to problems.

IT'S YOUR TIME TO STEP UP

Hopefully by now you see the value of self-leadership. It is not just a nice add-on to have, something that supplements your leadership ability. It is essential; it is pivotal. Trying to lead without being a strong self-leader is like getting into a car with no engine and wondering why you can't make it go.

The world is crying out for more self-leaders, more identity leaders. It's this type of leadership that is both lasting and impactful. It's this type of leadership that changes lives—yours and those of the people in your sphere of influence. It's this type of leadership from which legacies are made.

The great news is that anyone can learn to be an identity leader. This isn't for the chosen few. It's for anyone who cares to step into and master the type of leadership that is going to make a difference in the twenty-first century.

If you want to step into and master that type of leadership, keep reading. I'll show you how.

Trying to lead without being a strong self-leader is like getting into a car with no engine and wondering why you can't make it go.

Mastering others is strength. Mastering yourself is true power.
—LAO TZU

The Mark of a Self-Leader

A leader is best
When people barely know he exists.
Not so good when people obey and acclaim him.
Worse when they despise him.
But of a good leader, who talks little,
When his work is done, his aim fulfilled,
They will say:
We did it ourselves.

—Lao Tzu, sixth century BCE Chinese philosopher

IDENTITY LEADERSHIP KEYS

- The world is impacted and changed by leaders, not followers. Identity leadership is the highest order of leadership—the kind of leadership required in the twenty-first century.
- Self-leadership is a critical aspect of identity leadership. You have to learn how to lead yourself before you can learn to lead others.
- Identity leaders are problem solvers, bridge builders, and people connectors. They see and nurture the potential in themselves and in others.
- Identity leaders know who they are, where they are going, and how they are going to get there.
- Identity leaders are best prepared to take full advantage of the new opportunities that proliferate through the disruptive thinking taking place in industries and in every sector around the globe.

CHAPTER 2

Why Identity Matters

There is no easy journey to a great destination.

I was born in Whitesboro, New Jersey, one of six children. My father, Stedman Sr., was a painter, carpenter, and general contractor, and my mother, Mary, worked as a house cleaner and nurse's aide. We always had food on our table, presents under our Christmas tree, and love in our house.

I never felt we were poor. But some of my friends ate mayonnaise sandwiches—no meat, no cheese. Some shared a single bed with three or four other siblings. Some had holes in their walls.

My two younger brothers are developmentally disabled. Kids at school would make fun of us and call us names, and that stung. I began to develop shame and low self-esteem. I would get in fights and demand perfection of myself to prove to them that I was worth something.

Whitesboro was a black town inside a white county. The saying around there was "Nothing good ever came out of Whitesboro." That stung, too. We were proud that a relative of ours, George Henry White, was a leading investor who helped found the town, which was named after him. He was a lawyer and a congressman. He had made something of himself. But that connection, that pride, meant nothing to my schoolmates. When I transferred to an integrated school in sixth grade, I had to assimilate into a primarily white culture and deal with the idea that a lot of whites thought they were better than me just because of their skin color.

Race and skin color were big issues for me. They were a double-edged sword, one that I was cut by many times.

I determined I was going to prove my self-worth through basketball. I worked hard, scored over 1,000 points during my high school career, and was courted by a lot of college teams.

Maybe, I thought, something good could come out of Whitesboro after all.

I was recruited by UCLA, a perennial basketball power. They were in the midst of winning ten NCAA championships in twelve years—an amazing feat—led by their legendary coach John Wooden. The top team and the top coach in the nation wanted me to play for them.

I tell you, that was heady stuff for me back then. They flew me out to California. I met with the coaches and players, and they took me to Disneyland. On UCLA's campus, I saw my first cafeteria with all kinds of good food and was told to take whatever I wanted, however much I wanted.

I thought to myself, okay. *This* is living the life. I am finally living the life! I had to pinch myself to make sure I wasn't dreaming.

The plan was for me to go to UCLA after two years at a junior college. That plan never panned out.

I went to Weatherford Junior College in Weatherford, Texas, and started the journey that crisscrossed the country and then took me overseas and back again.

Weatherford dropped its basketball program after a year, so I transferred to the University of Detroit. But I never fit in there, didn't like the school, didn't see much playing time, and wanted out.

Harvey Catchings was a former teammate of mine at Weatherford.

Harvey went on to an eleven-year NBA career. He told me to join him at Hardin-Simmons University in Abilene, Texas. So I did. I ended up playing the rest of my collegiate career there, and graduated with a degree in social work.

While I had a degree, I didn't really know what I wanted to do with my life, other than play basketball. So I joined the army. I was stationed in Germany, where I worked as a hospital administrator—and, naturally, played for my service basketball team.

Some Germans told me they'd love for me to play for their club team. I ended up playing professionally in Europe for four years. I made some money, had some fun, and traveled throughout Europe. At least for a short time, I was living the life.

But when I came back to the States, I still didn't know what I wanted to do—because I still didn't know who I really was. My identity was pretty much as a basketball player at that point. But that portion of my life, at least as a professional, was coming to an end.

I took a career assessment test and scored in the ninety-ninth percentile for counseling and education, so I went to Ball State University and got a master's degree in education. That was a turning point for me. It helped crystalize my passion, which is to help people and educate them about their calling and identity.

It set me on the road to starting Athletes Against Drugs (AAD) in 1985. AAD is a nonprofit organization that provides services to youth. It has awarded millions of dollars in scholarships since its founding. And it led me in 1988 to creating my own company, S. Graham & Associates, a management and consulting firm that specializes in corporate and educational markets, producing resources and programs aimed at helping people in all walks of life develop their identity and leadership skills. Now I write books, give seminars, and take on speaking engagements, all with the focus of helping people discover their identities, their passions, and their talents. I help people become identity leaders.

When I was young and playing ball professionally in Europe, I thought I was living the life. But that life was short-lived. When I was back in the States, I realized my identity beyond basketball and embraced my real passion—helping and educating others, particularly in the areas of identity, self-development, and leadership—and I began living the life that I was meant to live.

And I haven't stopped since.

Becoming a leader is synonymous with becoming yourself. It is precisely that simple and it is also that difficult.

—WARREN BENNIS

YOUR IDENTITY JOURNEY

I've told you a bit of my journey so that you could see an example of how identity can form over time, how it unfolds and reveals itself through events and experiences and opportunities that come your way. I want to make this point very clearly: the identity process is unique for everyone. Yes, there is a process that we can use to uncover our identity and tap into our leadership capabilities—that general process remains the same. But how we experience that process is unique to each of us. So don't compare your own progress or experience to that of your friends or coworkers. Just focus on your own journey. That's really what this book is all about: helping you along on your own identity journey.

As you undertake that journey, you will be answering a lot of questions about yourself, your desires, your capabilities, your goals, and so on. But in a larger sense, all those questions will fit within these three overarching questions:

Who are you?

Where are you going?

How are you going to get there?

Let's spend a few minutes looking at each of those questions.

Who Are You?

A lot of people go through life without ever discovering who they truly are. They just fall into a pattern, a routine, a job, probably a series of jobs, and they do all of this more or less on autopilot, like a leaf floating downstream, going whichever way the current takes it. They don't think to ask themselves who they are, perhaps in part because they have no idea how to go about answering it. Some people don't want to know who they are, because they have low self-esteem and are afraid to uncover their true selves.

This is what I say to people who either think the question is too difficult to answer or who don't want to know the answer: *Finding out who you are at your core level is always—always—worth the effort.*

Who you are has to do with your talents, your abilities, your dreams, and your aspirations. No matter what your current situation is, no matter whether you are blue collar or white collar, no matter your neighborhood or race or religion or anything else, you have talents and abilities that give you innate pleasure when you use them—and in using them, you begin to show the world who you really are.

It is when we are fully operating in the gifts that we have been given that we are most fulfilled. And when we operate in those gifts, we come upon more opportunities, because the world opens up to us when it sees our full potential.

It is our obligation, then, to explore and understand what those gifts and talents are. And when we know them, when we understand what we are really motivated and energized to do and what gives us pleasure and happiness, when we are doing the thing we love and doing it with the abilities that we excel at, then we are poised to live to our full potential.

Identity leaders are able to tap into their full potential because they have the self-understanding to do so. But that self-understanding is just opening the door to your potential. The next step is figuring out what you want to do with that potential.

A lot of people go through life without ever discovering who they truly are. They just fall into a pattern, a routine, a job, probably a series of jobs, and they do all of this more or less on autopilot, like a leaf floating downstream, going whichever way the current takes it.

Where Are You Going?

Once you understand who you are, what your abilities are, what energizes you, and what holds the deepest meaning and value to you, then you can begin to form a vision for your life that centers on the fullest use of those talents and abilities. That vision is based on your self-understanding and your desires.

People are often challenged in this area by not dreaming big enough. They might understand their talents and have a grasp of what they want to do with those talents, but they are held back by fear ("Can I really do this?") or a false sense of humility ("I'm okay where I am; I should be satisfied with what I'm doing now") or shame ("people will laugh at me if I talk about a dream or a vision that I don't attain").

These kinds of people are most unhappy in life because deep down they know they want more and are capable of more. Understand that *more* doesn't mean more money or material goods or status or power. *More* in this instance means living a life where you fulfill your potential by doing the things that you do best and that energize you.

How Are You Going to Get There?

Once you know who you are and where you want to go, you need to figure out how you're going to get there. This stage is all about planning. You take the vision that you have formed and create a plan to realize that vision. That plan guides you along the way to realizing your full potential.

Such a plan takes the big picture, the end goal, the vision, and shapes it into something concrete and real, something challenging but attainable, something that has measurable steps and goals to get you to where you are functioning in your fullest capacity, doing what you do best, growing and expanding as you move along toward your vision.

You can see how your identity impacts all three of those questions. Understanding your identity is the key that unlocks the door to the answers for all of those questions. Your identity shapes your purpose. Your purpose shapes your plan. And your plan shapes your life.

The very essence of leadership is that you have to have a vision.
—THEODORE HESBURGH

Four key elements to your journey

As you undertake your identity journey, don't forget to:

- **Believe in yourself.** It doesn't matter what talents you have or dreams you harbor; if you don't believe in yourself, you won't tap into your full potential.

- **Know your competence.** Know what you are competent in now and what you want and need to gain competence in to realize your vision.
- **Continually challenge yourself.** Growth doesn't come without challenge. Stretch yourself; extend your boundaries. Identity leaders aren't afraid to fail. They use failure to grow more.
- **Be patient with yourself.** Growth, competence, opportunities, and realized dreams don't all come at once. They take time. Just keep at it; keep moving forward. Allow yourself to make mistakes and be flexible as you move toward your goals.

THE POWER OF IDENTITY

My entire purpose in writing this book and creating an identity leadership program is to help you embrace your passions and understand—and fulfill—your identity leadership capabilities. I want to help you live the life you were meant to live.

We all have the potential for greatness. Every one of us. The problem is, most of us don't know what our potential is, much less how to unlock it. Later in this book, I will take you through a process of unlocking that potential, realizing it, and packaging your purpose and passion to create a powerful life, one that energizes you and has you operating on all cylinders.

We all have the potential for greatness. Every one of us. The problem is, most of us don't know what our potential is, much less how to unlock it.

All of that hinges on identity. And Identity leads to self-leadership, and self-leadership opens up that life that you were meant to live.

When I ask most people what their identity is, they revert to what they *do*.

"I'm a teacher."

"I'm a sales associate."

"I'm a manager."

"I'm a baker."

"I own a flower shop."

That doesn't describe their core purpose in life, their innate abilities, their passions, their personalities, or their character traits. It describes what they do for a living. That's the external. I want to know their internal, what drives them, what makes them tick, what quickens their pulse. What would make them not hit their alarm and sigh as a new morning comes, but what would make them wake up before their alarm goes off, because they're so excited to start their day.

That latter type of person knows his identity. He knows what he's about, what he's doing, why he's doing it. And he can't wait to continue what he's doing.

That's where we all want to get.

Between grad school and starting my own business, I worked for a while in prison systems in Denver and Chicago. Prisons are filled with people who are there because they have no sense of who they are. They often have a fear-based, negative mindset and lack the skills to take charge of their own lives or emotions. They don't see any potential in themselves.

You might say, *Well, at least I'm not in prison.*

And I would counter with *You're in a prison of your own making if you don't know who you are and what your possibilities are. You may be free on the outside, but you are locked up on the inside.*

And that's no way to truly live.

IDENTITY LEADERSHIP KEYS

- Your identity forms over time, unfolding and revealing itself through events and experiences and opportunities that come your way. The general process is the same—but the specific experience is unique for everyone.

- It's not easy to uncover your core identity. But finding out who you are at your core level is always worth the effort. Realizing your identity will help you use your gifts and abilities to their fullest.

- Knowing your core identity means living a life where you fulfill your potential by doing the things that you do best and that energize you.

- You have the potential for greatness. Knowing your identity unlocks that potential so that you can live the life you were meant to live.

CHAPTER 3

Leaders, Not Labels

Refuse the labels that people use to define you and keep you in a box. The way out of that box is through self-leadership.

E arly in life, I let other people define me. I let people define me by my race. I came from a place that "nothing good came out of." I had two developmentally disabled brothers. I was an athlete. Though tests showed I had a high IQ, I was an average student with poor study habits.

I heard all this, I took it all in, and it confused me. I wanted more out of life, I wanted to make something of myself—to let people know something good could come out of Whitesboro—but I didn't know what. I couldn't make plans for my life because I had no concept of who I was or what I was capable of or even what I wanted to do, beyond basketball.

But over time, through a lot of trial and error, a lot of reading and soul searching, I did find out who I was. I figured out where I wanted to go. And I made a plan for how I was going to get there.

I found out that what truly matters is my ability to define myself based on understanding and then living out my passions. You have that ability, too. You can create a life that you want based on your own passions and strengths, not on someone else's ideas of who you are or what you should do.

I found out that what truly matters is my ability to define myself based on understanding and then living out my passions. You have that ability, too. You can create a life that you want based on your own passions and strengths, not on someone else's ideas of who you are or what you should do.

DON'T LET OTHERS LABEL YOU

It all hinges on how you define yourself and who determines that definition: you or someone else.

Without an identity, we allow ourselves to be defined by others. We are put in a box and labeled by race, gender, family circumstances, job title—the list of labels gets very long when other people define you.

When we are labeled and we accept those labels, we develop a mindset of inequality, which leads to us making poor choices and limiting our own potential and opportunities. The challenge is to get past the labels, to be able to focus on what's relevant to building our lives, what choices we should be making to achieve success based on our vision for ourselves.

But of course, we can't have that vision, we can't focus on what's relevant, if we don't know who we are. So again, you see the critical importance of understanding your identity.

When we buy into labels, we allow ourselves to be placed in a box, enslaved by what others think of us. The world says to us, *You don't know who you are. Let me tell you who you are.* The challenge is this: we need to shun the external labels that control our minds, take back our power and control, and define ourselves from the inside out.

HOW DO YOU THINK AND FEEL ABOUT YOURSELF?

I want to teach you how to change the way you think and feel about yourself. Because when you change your thoughts, you change your feelings—and when you change your feelings, you change your attitude.

And when you change your attitude, you change your life.

That first step—how you think and feel about yourself—is the most critical.

If you let others tell you who you are and what you are capable of, you are, in effect, their prisoner. They rule your life. They set your limits. They tell you how to view yourself and your place in this world.

That's what happens when you let others label you.

"But that's not who I really am!" a tiny voice inside you cries.

But unless you show the world who you really are, they won't believe any protests you raise.

The world, by default, will define you if you don't define yourself. The world will slap an identity on you, and it will never be a reflection of your true identity, capabilities, and gifts; it will always be a lesser, more restricted version of yourself. Or worse, it will be a completely false version of yourself.

The world will define you if you don't define yourself.
The world will slap an identity on you, and it will never
be a reflection of your true identity, capabilities, and
gifts; it will always be a lesser, more restricted version
of yourself. Or worse, it will be a completely false
version of yourself.

CREATING A LIFE BASED ON YOUR PASSIONS AND STRENGTHS

We all have the ability to create a life based on our passions and
strengths, rather than on someone else's ideas of who we are or what
we should do. Our first step toward that freedom is to discover who
we are. Then we can clearly articulate our vision, make good decisions, and begin to form habits that support our ongoing process as
we live out our identities.

With experience—mistakes included—our purpose and mission
emerge, and we gain in confidence as we realize we are living the life
we were meant to live.

I grew up in a time when racial segregation and discrimination
were legal. Think about that for a moment. It was not only accept-
able to erroneously label and restrict me; it was the social and cultural
norm to do so.

It is still the cultural norm to slap all kinds of negative labels on
people, labels that relate to race, religion, sexual identity, politics,
socioeconomic status, personal history, past mistakes, and so on.

You cannot get free of those labels until you develop a new clear
and accurate self-image.

Sidney Weinberg: From Janitor's Assistant to Top Boss at Goldman Sachs

Sidney Weinberg, one of eleven children, dropped out of school when he was in junior high. In the early 1900s, he started working at Goldman Sachs, an investment firm, as a janitor's assistant, making $3 per week brushing the firm partners' hats and cleaning their overshoes.

But one of the Sachs—the grandson of the founder—saw something in Weinberg. He promoted Weinberg to the mailroom, and Weinberg, who lacked education but not confidence, immediately reorganized the mailroom.

Weinberg rose through the firm until he became a partner in 1927. Three years later he became a senior partner, and that same year he became head of the firm, saving it from bankruptcy during the Great Depression. He remained head of Goldman Sachs until his death in 1969.

Sidney Weinberg knew who he was and what he was capable of. He knew himself so well that his capabilities quickly became apparent to the top people in the company. Despite his lack of education, his life was transformed from the lowest-paying job in the company to the highest, because he knew who he was.

George Washington Carver: No Obstacle Could Stop His Purpose

George Washington Carver was born into slavery during the Civil War. Talk about surviving and eventually thriving against the odds: all eleven of Carver's siblings died prematurely.

After slavery was abolished, Carver was raised by his former slave owners, who took him in as their own child. He faced many hardships in finding schools that would take blacks. But he loved education and clung fiercely to his vision of educating others. (In later years, he recalled a woman who told him, when he was renting a room from her to attend a school for black children, "You must learn all you can, then go back out into the world and give your learning back to the people.")

When he applied to a college and was accepted, he went there only to be turned away when they discovered he was black. He eventually attended Simpson College in Indianola, Iowa, and then Iowa State in Ames. He later became the first black faculty member at Iowa State, and he taught for forty-seven years at the Tuskegee Institute. Over the years, he conducted crop and agricultural research that bettered the lives of poor farmers, and he developed about 100 products made from peanuts, including cosmetics, dyes, paints, plastics, gasoline, and nitroglycerine. In later life, he became widely celebrated for his achievements.

Carver faced numerous obstacles throughout his life, especially early on. But he pressed forward. The obstacles temporarily slowed him at times, but he always got around them. He was determined to live the life he was meant to live. He knew his capabilities. He knew he was meant for education and research, and, as that woman early in his life had encouraged him to do, he gave his learning back to the people.

SCRIPT YOUR OWN LIFE

Think of your life as a story. As you live out your life, you are telling your story to the world. Just as stories do, our lives have twists and turns in them, plot points that can make our stories go in different directions.

We have the power to write our life's script. That doesn't mean we won't experience disappointments and challenges along the way; in fact, stories are made all the richer and more satisfying when we learn how people persevered in spite of those challenges and overcame them.

It's very freeing when we realize that our success in life is based on our ability and willingness to be the creators of our own future, to take ownership of our life. It's easy to look to external sources, to people and political or social organizations and other external forces, to change our life for us. But our greatest resource for changing our life does not lie in the outside world. It lies, instead, within us.

It's very freeing when we realize that our success in life is based on our ability and willingness to be the creator of our own future, to take ownership of our life.

As Mahatma Gandhi said, "You must be the change you wish to see in the world." In other words, if you change yourself, you will change the world.

However, change won't happen if we keep doing the same things that we have always done. It's easy to get stuck in routines and then get frustrated by the very fact that we are stuck in those routines.

Insanity has been described as doing the same thing over and over again and expecting different results.

We don't have to keep doing the same things over and over again. In fact, we can't do the same things over and over again if we want and expect change. We need to not only know ourselves and our passions, but take responsibility for them and pursue them in ways that necessitate change.

Until a book is completed, an author always faces a blank page just beyond what he or she has written so far. So it is with your life.

Today is a blank page. What are you going to write on that page? Next week, next month, next year, are blank pages. What will you write on them? And what labels will you have to strip yourself of, what self-image and self-understanding will you have to arrive at, to make the words dance off those pages?

It's up to you.

And after you finish this book, you will have the tools and the knowledge to start scripting.

If you hear a voice within you say, "You cannot paint," then by all means paint and that voice will be silenced.

—VINCENT VAN GOGH

Nelson Mandela: Never Losing Sight of His Identity

Nelson Mandela never lost sight of who he was.

A South African anti-apartheid revolutionary, Mandela was imprisoned for twenty-six years before being released by President F. W. de Klerk amid growing national and international pressure.

Mandela, whether freed or in prison, remained what he was: a born leader, a freedom fighter, and a man who stood for compassion, justice, and peace at all costs.

He represented himself at his initial trial and called no witnesses; instead, he gave a reasoned and passionate three-hour speech, titled "I Am Prepared to Die." Its message of equality, freedom, and democracy stirred and inspired people around the world. It is considered one of the great speeches of the twentieth century and a key moment in the history of South African democracy.

His speech was so titled because this is how he ended it:

> During my lifetime I have dedicated my life to this struggle of the African people. I have fought against white domination, and I have fought against black domination. I have cherished the ideal of a democratic and free society in which all persons will live together in harmony and with equal opportunities. It is an ideal for which I hope to live for and to see realised. But, My Lord, if it needs be, it is an ideal for which I am prepared to die.

"My Lord" refers to the judge who could have sentenced Mandela to death.

You can be sure that Nelson Mandela was firm in his own identity and sense of leadership. Nothing—not imprisonment or even the possibility of death—could shake him from that understanding or jar that self-image. He knew who he was and what he was made for, and four years after being freed, he was elected president of South Africa, the country's first black head of state and the first to be elected in a fully representative democratic election. But even before he became president, he met with many heads of state around the world, garnering worldwide support to end apartheid and institutionalized racism in South Africa. Apartheid was indeed ended in a series of steps in the early 1990s that culminated in Mandela's election as president.

The white-ruled Nationalist Party in South Africa tried to beat Mandela, but Mandela refused to be beaten. They tried to silence

Mandela, but he refused to be silenced. They tried to strip him of his power and dignity and identity, but he refused to be stripped. They tried to derail the legacy that he was building, but that legacy only grew. They tried to stop him from communicating, and the whole world heard his voice. They tried to build the walls of apartheid higher, but Mandela broke down those walls.

Nelson Mandela never lost sight of who he was or what his purpose was. And because of that, he brought justice and healing to an entire country.

A genuine leader is not a searcher for consensus but a molder of consensus.

—MARTIN LUTHER KING JR.

A LIFE OF PURPOSE AND PASSION

When we go through life without a plan or purpose, we create a survival mentality. We have no vision for ourselves, we burn out, we're not motivated, we can't find our way, and we don't know where to start.

Identity is a starting point. When we focus on what's important, we don't become victims of the external things that get in our way and marginalize our existence. With an identity, we start to act with purpose and clarity and receive insights that propel us forward.

Success flows from understanding who you are. Success is the end result of gaining a clear understanding of your identity, discovering what you love to do, and learning how to do it so well that you create value in the world. Your happiness and success in life flow from knowing who you are and establishing your authentic identity—first inside yourself, then externally in the world.

Success flows from understanding who you are. Success is the end result of becoming clear about your identity, discovering what you love to do, and learning how to do it so well that you create value in the world.

You have a unique life purpose. You have unique gifts and talents. You must learn how to dig deep inside of yourself and stop looking outside for your identity. Until you realize what is on the inside of you, your true talents will never add value to the lives of others. You will never fulfill your promise.

This book and my identity leadership program are aimed at helping you fulfill your promise and helping you live a life of purpose and passion.

One of the lessons I learned from successful people is that no matter where we come from, no matter our physical circumstances or any other turn of events, we're limited only by our own thinking and choices.

There are no guarantees in this world. Life is unpredictable, so your greatest asset is yourself. You can't control the world or what happens to you. But you can control how you respond to the world and to what happens to you.

To do that, though, and to be successful in doing it, especially in times of upheaval, you have to have a strong sense of self.

IDENTITY LEADERSHIP KEYS

- Create a life based on your own passions and strengths, not on someone else's ideas of who you are or what you should do.
- If we don't define ourselves, others will do it for us. And when we accept those labels, we limit our potential and opportunities. We need to shun the external labels, take back our power and control, and define ourselves from the inside out.

- Our lives are an ever-unfolding story. Don't let others write your story for you; take up the pen and write your own story. You are the creator of your own future. It's time to take full ownership of your life.
- Identity is the starting point of living a life of purpose and passion. Once you become aware of who you are and what's possible for you, you are limited only by your own thinking and choices.

CHAPTER 4

Identity Leaders of Today

Leadership is creating daily habits that support your life skills. It's doing the small things right.

In speaking to the plebe class at the United States Military Academy at West Point in 2009, author and essayist William Deresiewicz put it bluntly:

> We have a crisis of leadership in this country, in every institution....What we have now are...people who have been trained to be incredibly good at one specific thing, but who have no interest in anything beyond their area of expertise. What we *don't* have are leaders....People who can think for themselves. People who can formulate a new direction: for the country, for a corporation or a college, for the Army—a new way of doing things, a new way of looking at things. People, in other words, with *vision*.[6]

A recent Gallup study of 30,000 college graduates in the US shows that 25 percent of all college graduates fail to thrive in their lives and careers because college did not prepare them emotionally or experientially for the real world.[7] These graduates had lesser degrees of workplace engagement and well-being, leading to lesser productivity, greater absenteeism, and greater healthcare costs for companies, among other negative outcomes.

In a related study, Gallup found that American businesses lose $450 to $550 billion a year, because 70 percent of their workforce is not engaged and does not work at their full potential.[8]

In its 2014 Global Human Capital Trends survey, Deloitte found that leadership remains the top human capital concern—and presents the largest "readiness gap" in the survey.[9] The survey uncovered a deep need to develop new leaders faster and to globalize leadership programs. Eighty-six percent of respondents in the survey cited the leadership issue as "urgent" or "important." The report stated that twenty-first-century leadership is different, and that a shortage of leaders is one of the biggest impediments to growth.

The survey also found that companies face challenges in developing millennials and multiple generations of leaders in meeting the growing demand for leaders with global fluency and flexibility. The survey noted additional challenges in identifying leaders who can innovate and inspire others to perform, and who can understand the rapidly changing technologies and resulting new disciplines and fields.

The need for leadership will never go away. The premium on leadership will never be devalued, because leadership is the heartbeat of any company or organization. Every strong company has a strong leader and leadership team at the helm. Every one. And every company is looking to develop new and strong leadership, men and women who are capable of leading them in the next generation of their business. Companies are looking for people with vision and foresight and the complex leadership skills to take the company to the next level, maneuver successfully in the marketplace, and create growth and stability.

The world is calling for leaders. And there is no reason you can't answer that call.

But to best answer that call, you need to bring identity into the picture. That's one of the reasons that companies are saying leadership is in a critical state—too many people are focused on trying to develop leadership skills without coupling those skills with a deep and robust understanding of their identity.

The world is calling for leaders. And there is no reason you can't answer that call.

When you bring a complete and sure understanding of your identity to the leadership picture, you will stand out as a true leader who has much to offer. It's the marriage of identity and leadership that sets you apart as a twenty-first-century leader.

Why is that identity piece so powerful and so necessary?

It's because when we don't know who we are and what our capabilities are, we default to allowing others to label us. Those labels box us in and limit us. And those limitations mean we will never reach our full potential—including as leaders.

Throughout the rest of this chapter I'm going to introduce you to a handful of exemplary leaders in the world of business and sports who epitomize what it means to be an identity leader.

The secret of leadership is simple: Do what you believe in. Paint a picture of the future. Go there. People will follow.

—SETH GODIN

TOM BRADY: MAKING EVERY MOMENT COUNT

Tom Brady has put together a Hall of Fame National Football League career and is at the center of the discussion about who is the best quarterback of all time. And he is still going strong at age forty-one in the 2018 season, his eighteenth as a starting quarterback for the New England Patriots.

Brady has won six Super Bowls—the only player to ever do so—and has gone to the Pro Bowl, the all-star game for football, thirteen times. He has been NFL MVP three times and Super Bowl MVP four times, the most ever for a player, and in his first eighteen years as a starter, the Patriots won fifteen division titles, the most for any quarterback in history. He currently ranks fourth in passing yards, third in touchdown passes, and fourth in career passing rating. He has a slew of other records, both regular season and Super Bowl, that are too lengthy to go into here. Suffice it to say that he has excelled at the highest levels for nearly two decades in a very challenging sport. And that excellence has not diminished with age, as he is the oldest player to win a Super Bowl MVP at age thirty-nine and the oldest to win a regular-season MVP at forty.

Let me tell you a little story that gives some insight into how Tom Brady got to where he is. When he was a freshman at the University of Michigan, he was seventh on the quarterback depth chart. He was getting two repetitions—chances to practice—out of every fifty in practice. A psychologist told him something both simple and profound: stop focusing on the number of reps you're getting and start focusing on making them the best reps you can.

He adopted that mindset—that every rep counts—and in doing so he began to stand out. He got more and more reps in practice and he climbed up the depth chart all the way to number 1.

That's part of his success: determination, motivation, focus. But there is more to what he has been able to accomplish in the NFL.

Brady gets a lot of accolades, and deservedly so. But he is the first to admit that football is a team sport, and he is as focused on connecting with teammates and motivating them as he is on developing his own skills. Some of the players on his team are nearly twenty years younger than he is, but he makes a conscious effort to connect with them. And he knows that what motivates one type of teammate won't motivate another type. He treats his teammates as individuals, communicates a consistent message to them all, and exudes confidence and professionalism on and off the field. He is the consummate role model and leader.

Tom Brady has done it all on the field. No one in the history of the game has accomplished what he has as the field general of the New England Patriots. The work ethic that carried him from number 7 on the depth chart at Michigan to number 1 has carried him to the top of the football world—yet he continues to push himself to improve, learn, and motivate those around him.

SHERYL SANDBERG: ENGAGING OTHERS

Sheryl Sandberg is an exceptional leader, one of the best and brightest in America. In 2018, she was ranked number 6 on the 50 Most Powerful Women in Business list by *Fortune* and number 11 on *Forbes'* 2018 list of the 100 Most Powerful Women in the World. That type of ranking has been commonplace for her over the last decade as she has proven her leadership abilities over and over—as chief of staff for US secretary of the treasury Lawrence Summers; as vice president of global online sales and operations for Google (where she also launched Google's philanthropic arm, Google.org); for Facebook, where she was the first woman on the company's board of directors and serves as chief operating officer. She serves on many boards, including those for Facebook, the Walt Disney Company, Women for Women International, and the Center for Global Development. She is also founder of Leanin.org, a nonprofit organization that inspires women and supports them in their efforts to reach their goals.

One aspect of Sandberg's leadership that stands out is her ability to relate to and engage with employees. Many executives at her level don't take the time to talk with the people in the trenches, but Sandberg does. And she doesn't talk *at* them, she talks *with* them and elicits their thoughts. She asks questions and listens to the responses. And in asking those questions, she begins productive discussions and debates that lead to breakthroughs. Those breakthroughs wouldn't happen if she didn't take the time to talk to her employees and encourage their ideas.

Another of Sandberg's sterling leadership qualities is her ability to be vulnerable and honest. When her husband died suddenly in 2015, her long note on social media about her feelings prompted 74,000 people to respond. The same can happen in a boardroom, a lunchroom, an office, a restaurant—anywhere. Being vulnerable and honest, far from being a sign of weakness, is a sign of your humanity, a sign that you are not afraid to communicate difficult and personal messages or to admit frailty and mistakes. This is actually a sign of healthy self-esteem and opens doors to greater communication and understanding.

One final example of leadership from Sheryl Sandberg: her Lean In Foundation, started to empower women in their leadership skills, has more than 33,000 Lean In Circles in 150 countries across the world. She is not just out to better herself. She is out to better others, give them a hand up, and help as many as possible reach their potential.

JEFF BEZOS: MAN ON A MISSION

When Jeff Bezos started Amazon in 1994, when the global internet was in its infancy, he established this mission statement: "Our vision is to use this platform to build Earth's most customer-centric company, a place where customers can come find and discover anything and everything they might want to buy online."

The execution of that vision has resulted in Amazon becoming the world's first $1 trillion company. Bezos has directed Amazon's ascension to the top by conveying that vision to employees and stakeholders, helping them catch that same vision and push in the same direction. Bezos, a brilliant ideas man himself, gives his employees space to innovate, control their own projects, come up with brilliant ideas, and execute them.

Bezos is also not afraid of failure. You might think that the world's richest man, in charge of the world's richest company, doesn't know what it means to fail. Actually, Bezos has invested in many companies and ventures that never panned out. A man of large vision, he is not afraid to take risks, explore, and push back boundaries. Sometimes those efforts didn't yield much for Bezos in terms of financial gain—in fact, they often resulted in financial loss—but he learned from failure and never stopped pushing forward with his vision.

Bezos is also not afraid of failure. You might think the world's richest man, in charge of the world's richest company, doesn't know what it means to fail. Actually, Bezos has invested in many companies and ventures that never panned out.

Another mark of great leadership that Bezos exhibits is his ability to hire the best people. He looks for people who are resourceful and innovative and are skilled leaders in their own right. His policy of promoting from within also acts as a great incentive for his employees.

Amazon under Bezos's leadership will never grow stale, because he will not allow it to. He uses the latest technology to his benefit, and he encourages his employees to think outside the box regarding the use of technology. That's how Amazon's one-click checkout was born—a group of employees developed a way to make an already fast checkout experience even faster.

Jeff Bezos focuses on maximizing resources, eliminating waste, and optimizing time. For example, he hates wasting time in meetings, so in lieu of many meetings, he encourages Amazon managers to send memos that can be digested quickly and efficiently, covering the topics that would have been covered in meetings.

WARREN BUFFETT: GOING AGAINST THE GRAIN

Warren Buffett, Berkshire Hathaway CEO and self-made billionaire, has motivated more than 160 billionaires to give away at least half of their wealth for philanthropic causes. Buffett balances optimism and realism in his annual shareholder letters and has the ability to inspire confidence even in trying times, such as during the Great Recession, when investments were falling apart. Buffett is honest above all and is not afraid to admit when Berkshire's performance has been poor. As a result, people trust him and are willing to take his advice. His honesty and integrity inspire that confidence.

Buffett's positive attitude also serves him well as a leader. People are naturally attracted to someone who has a positive outlook on life, and are more willing to listen to and follow that person. That outlook gives them hope and gets them on board more readily than with someone who projects pessimism.

Buffett has some other leadership qualities that make him stand out as well.

For one, he is not afraid to go against conventional wisdom. He has made numerous investments in which either the timing or the company he was investing in seemed to invite disaster. Most fund managers would have steered clear of such investments, but many of these "unwise" investments turned into extremely lucrative deals for Buffett. The point is he was not swayed by popular opinion; he carefully weighed his decisions and went forth with them regardless of what conventional wisdom would have him do.

Humility is another strong leadership feature of Buffett's. He is down-to-earth and affable, and when he took heat in the late 1990s for not investing in the tech sector, he replied that he "didn't invest in businesses he could not understand." It's the rare public figure who would admit a lack of knowledge in an area where people would assume he possessed knowledge. He has been quoted as saying that some of his managers are better at running Berkshire Hathaway than he is, and he has admitted to mistakes, such as not selling Tesco shares in a timely manner and for the decline of the jet rental company NetJets.

Buffett has a hands-off leadership style, allowing his managers to make their own decisions and manage their own businesses. But he is not hands-off in terms of giving praise; he regularly names many people for their hard work and accomplishments in his annual report to investors.

Through Warren Buffett's leadership, Berkshire Hathaway has become the world's eleventh-largest company, making over $200 billion a year. Regarding his own income, Buffett is the world's third-richest person, and he has pledged to give away 99 percent of his fortune to philanthropic causes.

Leaders walk a fine line between self-confidence and humility.
—STANLEY McCHRYSTAL

JOHN W. ROGERS JR: THE CONSUMMATE TEAM LEADER

John W. Rogers Jr. knows a lot about teamwork. He was captain of the 1979–1980 Princeton men's basketball team, which was co-champion of the Ivy League. He played under legendary coach Pete Carril, who preached the importance of team.

"The first lesson was about teamwork and caring about your teammates first," Rogers says. "He pounded it home and eventually it became such a freeing and fun way to play. There was a transformation. He no longer had to push the idea; the team fully embraced it. You're not thinking about who scores the points or who gets the credit; you're thinking instead about how you can help your teammate succeed on the court."[10]

Rogers has created a similar environment at Ariel Investments, which he founded in 1983 with $10,000. The company now manages over $11 billion and has earned investors a net annualized return of 10.71 percent since its inception.

"I constantly make sure we've created an environment that encourages people on the team to really say what they think, to get their ideas out on the table, and to give them the opportunity to argue those perspectives and make sure they're not holding them inside and going home and talking to their family about the idea," he says. "That's something I'm constantly working at; how can I create that environment, how can I ask the right questions, how do I go around and make sure people tell you what they really think? That takes patience, but it's the right thing to do."

Rogers's investment approach and wisdom—Ariel's motto is "Slow and steady wins the race"—has guided the company's success and branded Rogers as among the top 1 percent of money managers in the country. To say he has been successful as a businessman and company leader is an understatement.

But his influence does not stop with his business success. Rogers played a major fundraising role for Barack Obama leading up to the 2008 presidential election, and he was a leader of the 2009 inaugural committee. In addition, he has served on numerous boards of various corporations and of civic, educational, and arts organizations, including the Chicago Symphony Orchestra, the Rainbow/PUSH Coalition, and the Oprah Winfrey Foundation.

Like many leaders, Rogers is keenly interested in giving back, in opening up opportunities for people who would otherwise not have those opportunities. For example, he invests a lot of time, money, and energy in improving financial literacy among inner-city minority youths. In 1996, he started Ariel Community Academy in Chicago. The academy is a public school that focuses on financial education, teaching students the fundamentals of finance and investing. Rogers has long been a leader in youth education in Chicago, where he was born and raised.

It's not surprising that in 2008, Rogers became the first African American winner of a Woodrow Wilson Award from Princeton for his service to the Princeton alumni community, the Chicago community, the African American community, and the financial community.

MARY BARRA: AN INCLUSIVE TEAM BUILDER

When Mary Barra took over as CEO of General Motors in 2014, she immediately faced a crisis involving an ignition switch malfunction in one of GM's older vehicles. The malfunction had resulted in 124 deaths and 275 injuries. GM ended up recalling more than 30 million vehicles that year. Years later, Barra said that this experience changed her leadership style. She learned to be more insistent about addressing problems thoroughly and quickly. In doing so, she transformed GM's culture, which had become one where not many concerns were voiced, and if they were, they often didn't get far. She revamped management processes, creating a more transparent culture, and slowly won back trust from consumers.

Under Barra's leadership, even amid that recall scandal, GM broke its sales records in 2014. Since then, Barra has pushed GM into the technology space, including the driverless car space, with major acquisitions such as Strobe, a startup focused on driverless technology. She also pushed GM to develop the Chevy Bolt EV in 2017, beating Tesla in developing the first electric car priced under $40,000 with a range of 200 miles.

Barra is the first female CEO of a major global automaker. She has spent her entire career at GM, beginning at age eighteen as a co-op student, checking fender panels and inspecting hoods to pay for her college tuition.

Barra has a no-nonsense approach to leadership. When she was head of human resources at GM in 2009, she edited a ten-page dress code manual to two words: *Dress appropriately.* Rather than dictate to everyone what was appropriate, she empowered managers to do so.

Barra has a no-nonsense approach to leadership. When she was head of human resources at GM in 2009, she edited a ten-page dress code manual to two words: *Dress appropriately.* Rather than dictate to everyone what was appropriate, she empowered managers to do so.

But perhaps her defining attribute as a leader is her inclusiveness. She gives employees a voice and looks for diverse input on issues. She is a great listener and is approachable. After coming on board as CEO, she got GM's purchasing and product development departments to work together, something that had not been happening. She values transparency, honesty, communication, and teamwork, and she has created highly effective work teams in her tenure as CEO.

At the Wharton School's 2018 People Analytics Conference, Barra outlined eight principles of leadership that have led to her success:[11]

1. She consistently asks for feedback from those around her.
2. She holds meetings to discuss issues, not to have information shared. Pertinent information should be shared before the meeting and then discussed.
3. She keeps her message simple and clear—for example, "zero crashes, zero emissions." This is particularly important for larger organizations.
4. She effects sustainable change by making sure the benefit of that change is greater than the effort needed to pull it off.
5. She knows the ins and outs of her business. This helps her see how the parts relate and connect to each other.
6. She appeals to both hearts and minds—the emotions and the intellects—of her team.
7. She aligns her decisions with her values.
8. She leads by doing, not by saying. Her behavior helps determine the culture of GM.

Based on her success and on the principles by which she lives, it's not hard to see why Mary Barra is regularly ranked by *Forbes* as one of the world's most powerful women and, in recent years, was ranked number 2 and then number 1 by *Fortune* on their Most Powerful Women list.

HOWARD SCHULTZ: A PASSION FOR PEOPLE

Transformational leaders inspire others to develop their full potential as they pull together as a team working toward both common and individual objectives. Howard Schultz, chairman emeritus of Starbucks, embodies what transformational leadership is all about.

Schultz, who was CEO of Starbucks from 1986 to 2000 and from 2008 to 2017 (and its executive chairman from 2017 to 2018), is an enthusiastic and positive-minded leader who inspires workers to become team players, to be innovative problem solvers, and to be unafraid to voice their own views. (In fact, this is how the Frappuccino was created—it came from one of his employees.) He invests his time and energy in his employees, knowing that people who are motivated and given responsibility will blossom and take a business to higher levels. He invests in them in other ways, too: with comprehensive health insurance, the option to own stocks (even for part-time employees), tuition benefits, shifting schedules, and other perks and bonuses, financial and otherwise.

Schultz is a great believer in diversity and in respecting different cultures, and this plays out in how Starbucks is managed, how it chooses and works with its suppliers, and how Starbucks invests in the economic development of communities.

He once told Oprah Winfrey on her talk show that his passion was in building a company that treats people with respect and dignity. That vision, from the leader of the company, makes a tremendous impact in what employees think about their work and how they approach their customers.

Schultz grew Starbucks from a tiny Seattle company to one with more than 23,000 outlets in seventy-two countries. He made the most of the opportunities he was given—or that he created for himself. For example, it took a year for the original Starbucks owners to hire him, and when he saw great potential in expanding into the café business—Starbucks at first just sold roasted coffee beans—his ideas were rejected. So, he left Starbucks, opened his own chain of coffee bars, and eventually went back and bought Starbucks, merging it with the chain he had started.

That's tenacity, vision, discipline, courage, passion, and many other traits—all components of Schultz's leadership style.

When most people think of Starbucks, they think of coffee or coffee-related products. Not Howard Schultz. Schultz thinks of people. He has said, "Coffee is what we sell as a product, but it's not the business we're in. We're in the people business. I'm passionate about the human connection."

KEVIN WARREN: RESILIENT AND VISIONARY

Kevin Warren spent several months in a body cast after a car hit his bicycle when he was twelve years old. He had no TV in his hospital room; he was just alone in his bed with his thoughts.[12] The seeds of resiliency had surely been planted before then, but during that time in the hospital those seeds sprouted. He developed the determination, mental toughness, and optimism that would carry him, beyond all odds, not just through that experience but through a life filled with achievement.

Warren was warned by his doctor that once he was free from his cast, he might never walk again. He asked the doctor what would give him the greatest chance of recovery. The doctor responded, "Swimming." So Warren told his parents he wanted to build a swimming pool in his back yard, paid for with the settlement he received from the driver who injured him.

He swam so much that he all but developed gills. Did he recover?

Well, he went on to a collegiate basketball career at the University of Pennsylvania, where he averaged twenty points per game as a freshman, the fourth-highest single-season average in the school's history.

A Tempe, Arizona, native, Warren transferred to Grand Canyon University in Phoenix, where he scored 1,118 points over his final three years and earned Academic All-America honors. He was inducted into the university's Athletics Hall of Fame, only the fifth basketball player to receive that prestigious honor.

So, yes, he recovered—quite nicely.

But he didn't stop after earning his bachelor's in business administration. He went on to earn an MBA from Arizona State University and a JD from the University of Notre Dame. He is a licensed attorney in three states and the District of Columbia.

Warren has been an executive in the National Football League since 1997, first with the St. Louis Rams, then the Detroit Lions, and, since 2005, with the Minnesota Vikings. In 2015, he became chief operating officer (COO) for the Vikings; he is the highest-ranking African American executive working on the business side for an NFL team and the league's first-ever black COO. In 2017, he received the inaugural Texas Southern University Pioneer Award for breaking a major barrier for blacks in the NFL.

Warren's leadership abilities have resulted in him being named to numerous committees, boards, and councils. Under his leadership, the Vikings have developed leadership initiatives, implemented platforms on positive community impact, launched a women's initiative program, and created an elevated fan experience.

Warren is truly a visionary leader whose drive, determination, and optimism know no bounds. He sees the potential in people and calls it out, helping them to develop to their full abilities. In every challenge he encounters, he sees the possibilities and opportunities that can result in overcoming the challenge. And then he plots how to overcome the challenge, just as he did when he got out of that body cast and got into the swimming pool that was built with his own money.

A leader sees the potential in people and calls it out, helping them to develop to their full abilities.

Warren has another great attribute as a leader: compassion. He and his wife, Greta, have donated more than 3,600 backpacks to Lucy Craft Laney Community School in Minneapolis, a school they "adopted" that has 98 percent of its students coming from under-served communities. And in 2014, the Warrens donated $1 million to a pediatric emergency care assistance fund in honor of Warren's sister Carolyn Elaine Warren-Knox, who died of brain cancer the previous year. The Warrens also started a scholarship program for high school seniors who will be first-generation college students, awarding $5,000 annual scholarships to sixteen students each year.

When Warren was in the ambulance after his bike accident, a nurse helped keep him alive and comforted him. Three weeks later, she visited him in the hospital and said, "I knew you would make it. I hope you have a good life."

Kevin Warren has lamented that he has never been able to find that nurse to thank her for the encouragement. But he has had a great life—and he has certainly passed the message of encouragement he received from that nurse on to those he has met on his life's journey.

If you can dream it, you can do it. Always remember that this whole thing was started with a dream and a mouse.

—WALT DISNEY

SAFRA CATZ: DRIVEN, STRATEGIC, APPROACHABLE

Safra Catz is a driven, organized, energetic, and productive leader. The CEO of Oracle Corporation, a multinational computer technology company, Catz has several times been listed among the most powerful women in business by both *Forbes* and *Fortune* and is the highest-paid female CEO of any US company. She was elected to the board of directors of the Walt Disney Company in 2017 and was considered by President Donald Trump for a post in his administration. She also is a lecturer in accounting at the Stanford Graduate School of Business. And from 2008 through 2015, Catz was a director of HSBC Holdings, a British multinational banking and financial services holding company. She has been an executive at Oracle since 1999 and a board member since 2001 and was named co-president and CFO in 2011 before being named CEO three years later.

Catz is known as a leader who values teamwork, collaboration, and a clear business strategy. She communicates that strategy consistently and inspires employees to embrace the strategy. She also empowers her employees by listening to their ideas and viewpoints, challenging or exploring those viewpoints, and letting people make decisions and execute them. She is not afraid to change her position based on new facts, and it is this attitude that encourages employees to express their ideas.

Safra Catz is reputed not to like the spotlight. But the spotlight likes her. It's difficult to stay out of it when you are such an influential and successful leader.

BILL GATES: EMPOWERING OTHERS

Every leader is much more complex than the descriptions offered in these short profiles, and Bill Gates is a great example of that. It's difficult to capture the inner workings of a leader in a few short paragraphs. Every leader has his own strengths and weaknesses, and for many of these leaders, those strengths and weaknesses—or those leadership attributes that sometimes seem to contrast with and contradict one another—are displayed for the world to see.

For example, Bill Gates, principal founder of Microsoft Corporation, was often difficult to communicate with. He could be verbally combative in meetings, and he also could be authoritarian, autocratic, and demanding.

Yet he was also visionary and charismatic. He knew how to inspire positive change, he knew when to support and encourage people in their ideas, and despite his at times abrasive leadership style, he ultimately gained the deep trust and respect of his managers.

Gates is often compared to the late Steve Jobs, cofounder of Apple, Inc. But whereas Jobs was a lone wolf, Gates valued input from his employees. He believed in building strong teams and in delegating tasks.

One of his greatest attributes as a leader was his ability and drive to think big. Back in 1980, just a handful of years after founding Microsoft, Gates pronounced the company's vision: "A computer on every desk in every home." That seemed outlandish and preposterous at the time. But now, close to 90 percent of households in the US have at least one computer.

Gates has a number of other exemplary attributes as a leader. He looks beyond the present and is constantly conceiving of ways to improve on what is already good. He sets large goals and then drives methodically and relentlessly toward them. When he was still in a leadership role at Microsoft (he left in 2014 to focus on his work at the Bill & Melinda Gates Foundation), he stimulated creativity and growth in his employees. He sees learning as an ongoing, lifelong process; he is constantly learning and evolving. He once said, "Your most unhappy customers are your greatest source of learning."

Gates is also committed to giving back. His philanthropic work through his foundation and elsewhere is a model for all leaders to aspire to. He founded the Giving Pledge with Warren Buffett in 2009 to encourage billionaires to pledge at least half of their wealth to philanthropy.

His foundation has donated billions of dollars to causes all over the world. His life has been about more than making a profit. It's been about making a difference in people's lives—whether through the products Microsoft has generated or through giving resources to help people in need.

In short, Bill Gates is a master at empowering others.

Time named Gates one of the 100 people who most influenced the twentieth century as well as one of the 100 most influential people of 2004, 2005, and 2006 (he was *Time*'s co-Person of the Year in 2005). He was made an Honorary Knight Commander of the Order of the British Empire by Queen Elizabeth II in 2005 and was presented, along with Melinda Gates, with the Presidential Medal of Freedom by President Obama in 2016 for their philanthropic work. In 2017, he and Melinda were similarly presented France's highest national award, the Legion of Honour, for their charity efforts.

A leader is a master at empowering others.

THE TAKE-HOME MESSAGE

The people profiled in this chapter make up an amazing assortment of leaders. Hopefully you received a glimpse into the character, personality, and attributes that have helped make them so successful. I want to make a few points about these leaders and about leadership in general:

- Leaders are individuals. Each leader has his or her own strengths and weaknesses.
- Leadership is not a formula or recipe. People with very different styles and personalities can be great leaders. There is no one leadership style that all leaders use.

- There are, however, some attributes that most leaders tend to share. Those include vision, passion, motivation, team building, perseverance, discipline, optimism, communication skills, honesty, and not being afraid of failure.

I hope this chapter acts as a mirror for you—one you can hold up to yourself and see your own positive leadership attributes, as well as areas that you want to grow in. The goal here is not to be the next Jeff Bezos or Bill Gates; it's to be the best version of you that you can be.

IDENTITY LEADERSHIP KEYS

- Leadership is a need that will never go away. The premium on leadership will never be devalued, because leadership is the heartbeat of any company or organization. Every strong company has a strong leader and leadership team at the helm. Every one. And every company is looking to develop new and strong leadership, men and women who are capable of leading them in the next generation of their business.
- When you bring a complete and sure understanding of your identity to the leadership picture, you will stand out as a true leader who has much to offer. It's the marriage of identity and leadership that sets you apart as a twenty-first-century leader.
- The goal is not to emulate any of the leaders in this chapter. The goal is to be inspired by them to be the best version of you that you can be.

CHAPTER 5

Oprah: A True Identity Leader

Oprah has a strong sense of self, a drive and an ambition, to empower people around the world. She is willing to take a stand for what she believes in. I've seen her do that over and over again when she didn't know what the outcome would be.

No one is better qualified as an identity leader than Oprah Winfrey. Oprah sets the standard. She has climbed to the pinnacles of success from the humblest of origins, from a life of poverty and racism in the Deep South, because she always knew who she was. She always believed in herself, and she always remained focused on her goals, on her development as a person, a leader, and later as a role model for people all over the world.

Think of this: She was born to an unwed teenager. She had no father in her home. For her first six years of life, she lived not with her mother but with her maternal grandmother, who was often forced to clothe her in dresses made of potato sacks because they were so poor. She was molested by several people beginning at age nine. At thirteen, she ran away from home. At fourteen, she gave birth to a son who was born prematurely and died shortly after birth.

These are not the normal underpinnings of success. Given that background, the typical person would not grow into the woman, the leader, the philanthropist, that Oprah became. If Hollywood wrote a script about a story like hers, it would be turned down for being out-landishly unrealistic.

"THE ABILITY TO TRIUMPH BEGINS WITH YOU"

So how did she overcome all of that? How did she get to where she is today? As she says, "It doesn't matter who you are, where you came from. The ability to triumph begins with you. Always."

That is the core of identity leadership right there. *The ability to triumph begins with you. Always.*

Born in Mississippi, moved to Milwaukee, Wisconsin, at the age of six, to Nashville, Tennessee, two years later. Then she moved back to Milwaukee as a teenager, where she was constantly ridiculed for her poverty. Back to Nashville. She moved so much that it's amazing she didn't get whiplash.

And yet, the idea that the ability to triumph begins with you took root in her at an early age. It not only took root; it began to bloom, despite her circumstances. When she was nineteen, a sophomore in college, she became the youngest and first African American anchor for WTVF-TV in Nashville. She began her climb in the media, anchoring *A.M. Chicago*, which aired opposite Phil Donahue; the following year, in 1985, the show was renamed *The Oprah Winfrey Show*. That show ran for twenty-five years, with 4,561 episodes during which she interviewed 30,000 guests. It was aired in 145 countries. The show received 20 million letters over the years.

It was an amazing run by an amazing woman.

And that just scratches the surface of her accomplishments and who she is.

She is an actress, having been nominated for an Academy Award for her role in *The Color Purple*. She has acted, voiced, produced, and directed numerous films and shows. She has coauthored five books. She created Oprah.com, which gets more than 70 million page views and more than 6 million users per month. She publishes magazines. In 2018, she signed a multiyear deal with Apple to create original programming.

She has topped lists by CNN and *Time* as being the world's most powerful woman. She has been tapped as the most influential woman in the world by numerous other media, and as one of the 100 people who most influenced the twentieth century by *Time*. She has appeared on *Time's* "most influential people" list ten times, the only person to be named that many times.

GIVING BACK, OPENING PATHWAYS FOR OTHERS

Oprah has so many traits and characteristics of an identity leader. One of them is her willingness and desire to give back. She became the first black person to rank among the fifty most generous Americans. She has given away hundreds of millions of dollars to educational causes. When Hurricane Katrina destroyed thousands of homes in the southern US, she gave $10 million to the rebuilding of homes. In 2007, she opened the Oprah Winfrey Leadership Academy for Girls, a boarding school for girls in grades 8–12, in South Africa. She is helping them do exactly what she did: triumph over adversity. These girls are coming from shantytowns, from the kind of poverty that Oprah came from. Her academy is a beacon of hope for these girls. It is teaching them that they are capable, that they can overcome their circumstances, that they can create a good life based on their own identity and their own skills and aspirations. And that's what identity leaders do: they stoke the fires for those around them and under them, they instill confidence and hope, and they expand visions and goals.

Her goal with the academy is simple: to create a safe space to educate, nurture, empower, and inspire the next generation of leaders for South Africa and for the world.

Identity leaders have big visions, and those visions do not just impact themselves; they impact hundreds, thousands, perhaps even millions of people. The very essence of leading implies helping others, nurturing them, inspiring them. No one does those things like Oprah does.

Obviously, Oprah has impacted millions of people around the world. She has impacted me as well. We have been in a relationship since the mid 1980s, and I am a better person because of our relationship. When you are in a relationship with a woman who is routinely recognized as arguably the most influential and most powerful woman in the world, you are going to face a lot of scrutiny and challenges.

I'm a better person because I have had to do the work to define myself, to be who I am, as opposed to being defined by who she is. Sometimes people recognize me because of her, and that motivates me to work more on myself so I am not defined by our relationship. As I've said, it's not how the world defines you; it's how you define yourself. You have to figure out how to be yourself. That's what Oprah has done. Despite her difficult circumstances from the beginning of her life all the way through high school, she not only figured out who she was, but found a way to maintain her identity in the face of tremendous obstacles. She understood who she was and how to be who she was.

Leadership is not about titles, positions, or flow charts. It is about one life influencing another.

—JOHN C. MAXWELL

KEYS TO HER SUCCESS AS AN IDENTITY LEADER

Many people define success by how much money they make. Obviously, Oprah makes a lot of money, but that's not at the core of who she is or what she's about. That money is an outcome of her ability to position herself to fully use her talents.

People ask me what the key to her success is. Well, there are a lot of keys. At the core of it all is her understanding of her identity. She stays in her lane, making things relevant to who she is. She centers her life and lifestyle around the core of who she is. She focuses on the things she knows, the things she is passionate about, the things she loves. She doesn't pretend to know it all, and she doesn't care to know it all. She is an expert in her field, and she operates in her strengths and pursues her passions, which are based on her identity.

This is what I would say are some of the keys to her success—as an identity leader, as a businesswoman, as a philanthropist, as a person:

1. **She works hard.** She knows we cannot achieve our fullest without hard work.
2. **She is energetic.** She throws herself into her work, giving it her all. She is long past the point where she could coast, but she doesn't—because that's not her nature.
3. **She believes in and takes personal responsibility.** She believes we need to be accountable for our actions.
4. **She loves learning.** She is a tireless learner.
5. **She is not afraid to take risks.**

6. **She is not afraid of failure.** She's had plenty of failures in her life; she just learns from them and moves on. She says, "There's no such thing as failure in my life. I just don't believe in it. I have no fear of failure or of succeeding. I just do what I do, and I know that will keep me in the best place."

7. **She maintains a balance between her personal and professional life.** She manages stress on both sides of her life very well.

8. **She is honest and transparent.** As she says, "You can't know the truth until you're willing to know yourself—and vice versa. Knowing yourself is a lifelong process, with your biggest lessons often emerging from your biggest mistakes."

9. **She is decisive.** She gathers the facts and information she needs and moves forward with a decision based on her instincts.

10. **She adds value.** Her businesses, shows, and ventures are all about giving back to, not just taking from, customers or students or audiences.

11. **She loves herself.** Oprah has long valued healthy self-love and love of others. "It fills you up," she says. "It mends the tattered and broken spaces in your spirit. It makes you feel whole."

12. **She enjoys the journey.** This can be easier said than done for someone with her schedule, but she takes the time to enjoy successes and milestones along the way, as well as the daily journey. If she were not able to do this, she would have burnt out long ago.

You can't just sit there and wait for people to give you that golden dream. You've got to get out there and make it happen for yourself.

—DIANA ROSS

THE PROTOTYPICAL IDENTITY LEADER

As an identity leader, Oprah is well aware of the value of process. "The whole path to success is not as difficult as some people would want you to believe," she says. "The process was the goal. I've taken great joy in that process." That process, she adds, is a series of daily building blocks. "What you built yesterday should be linked to what you do today and tomorrow."

Oprah Winfrey was born to be a leader. She has the strongest sense of identity that I've ever seen, and how that identity is played out in her leadership has transformed and added value to millions of lives. She stays true to her values, and she speaks her mind with grace and composure. She is well prepared, intelligent, and quick on her feet. She can adjust on the fly and remain focused on the end goal, no matter the distractions or obstructions. For these and a host of other reasons, Oprah is the prototypical identity leader.

IDENTITY LEADERSHIP KEYS

- You have it within yourself to succeed and to be an identity leader. As Oprah says, "It doesn't matter who you are, where you came from. The ability to triumph begins with you. Always."
- Identity leaders know first how to lead themselves and then how to lead others—how to instill confidence and hope, expand visions and goals.
- Identity leaders have an innate sense of who they are and find a way to maintain their identity in the face of tremendous obstacles. Circumstances around them may change, but at their core, identity leaders do not change who they are.
- Identity leaders shape their lives around their core identity, focusing on what they are passionate about, what they love, and what their purpose is.

CHAPTER 6

How Identity Leaders Lead

Leaders work on improving themselves. They have the ability to get people to believe in their vision, because they believe in it themselves and are strong self-leaders.

Nelson Mandela was the epitome of an identity leader. Twenty-six years in prison did not alter who he was, and he ended up changing the course of history in South Africa. He went from reviled prisoner to revered president. He became a world leader because he never lost sight of who he was, he never gave up on his ideals or his purpose, and he never flinched in the face of decades-long struggles. Nelson Mandela was a man who knew himself inside and out, and of all the tremendous identity leaders I have had the pleasure to meet and know, he stands head and shoulders above the rest. He possessed so many of the characteristics a strong identity leader needs.

THE WORLD NEEDS IDENTITY LEADERS

When you look at social media, when you scan the news, when you listen to the talk shows on television and radio, it's easy to think that the world is populated not with people but with lemmings. People are constantly being pulled into other people's realities, often unthinkingly parroting others' views and opinions or simply following the trends and fads of the day.

The world needs self-leaders now more than ever. It's from self-leaders that the world gets its innovative ideas and creative solutions. Self-leaders aren't swayed by public opinion or pulled into other people's realities; they are firm in their own opinions and live lives of authenticity in their own realities.

They lead from who they are, which is the only way to successfully lead. And that style of leadership makes them stand out in a crowd of leaders.

Real leadership is leaders recognizing that they serve the people that they lead.

—PETE HOEKSTRA

STEPPING INTO YOUR ROLE AS AN IDENTITY LEADER

Leaders rise up—which means they weren't always leaders, but they transitioned into that role. How bumpy or smooth that transition is depends on various factors. I want to make four points here:

1. *Be aware that any ascension to a higher position with more responsibility and leadership is going to be accompanied by more stress, at least at the beginning.* Manage that stress in healthy ways—through appropriate exercise, nutrition, sleep, and balance in life—and seek out the wisdom of mentors or other leaders who can coach you and offer support and guidance.

2. *While it's likely that you have good communication skills, as someone in a leadership position, pour energy into enhancing those skills in your interactions as a new leader.* Listen to other

leaders and to those under you, empathize with them, express your ideas openly and clearly, invite the ideas of others, offer support where needed, and seek support where needed.

3. *Give yourself time to grow into the role.* You are in a leadership role because you have what it takes to lead—but remember that leaders are continually developing their skills, particularly their soft skills, or emotional intelligence. Successful leaders are those who invest in themselves. Leaders have to lead themselves first.

4. *Realize that identity leaders impact the world wherever they are.* That means you are the same person, with the same identity and leadership abilities, whether you are in your workplace, your home, your neighborhood, your place of worship, your social groups, your community, or anywhere else. You don't put on and take off an "identity leader hat"; you *are* an identity leader. You have the opportunity to impact people in positive ways wherever you are. Look for those opportunities.

Identity leaders impact the world wherever they are.

When you step into your role as an identity leader, you find yourself standing on a foundation for growth. Your vision for your life crystalizes. More opportunities come your way—because, in reality, you are in a position to see and receive them. Your potential begins to unfold and grow. What seemed like insurmountable problems before are solvable issues now. Your relationships—at work, at school, at home, in the community, everywhere—improve. People are attracted to your positive energy. You find a greater freedom to your expression, because you know who you are, what you are about, what your passions are, and what your purpose is. You enjoy life more.

HOW AN IDENTITY LEADER LEADS

Identity leaders lead from authenticity—meaning they are true to themselves and to the company's ideals and values. They don't ask of others what they don't ask of themselves. Their leadership is imbued with a strong and accurate sense of self and an unwavering confidence in their ability to succeed.

When problems arise and failures come, they do not point fingers. Instead, they persevere, they regroup, they arrive at solutions, and they learn from setbacks. They are not cowed by obstacles but are inspired by them to find solutions. They think for themselves and also welcome the ideas of those around them. They are not threatened by brilliant ideas of those under them; rather, they nurture and celebrate those brilliant ideas.

Identity Leaders Are Strong Communicators and Team Players

Identity leaders are strong communicators at all times— particularly when the waters are troubled. They can articulate clear missions and visions and plans and be a calming influence in times of turmoil.

Identity leaders are true team players, regardless of their position. They are not afraid to ask for help, ideas, or a critical analysis. Their focus is on the team mission and goal, and they hold themselves and others accountable in reaching those goals. As they work toward those goals, assessing a complex array of information, ideas, and solutions, they never lose sight of the overall vision of what they are charged with accomplishing.

Teamwork makes the dream work.

—JOHN C. MAXWELL

Identity Leaders Know Themselves Well

Identity leaders don't rely on past traditions or models that do not serve them well today. Instead, they "drill and dispel"—that is, they drill down to their core identity until they know themselves inside out, and they dispel what is irrelevant to them based on that core identity. Were you to sit down with an identity leader, she would be able to clearly and completely answer these questions: What motivates you in your work? What is it that you bring to your work that makes you stand out? What are your passions and strengths? What makes you tick?

In fact, knowing their passions and strengths helps them to navigate the choppy waters of the business world and helps them narrow the gap between where they are now and where they aim to be. And that is another defining factor of identity leaders: They know where they want to be. And they know how they are going to get there. They have a plan—a clear, concise, focused plan—that acts as a road map for their destinies. They have a success model that constantly evolves as they grow, expand their knowledge, improve their skills, and come upon new opportunities and experiences that will help them get to where they want to go.

Identity Leaders Develop Healthy Habits

Identity leaders not only know who they are; they develop habits that help them improve their abilities, gain the experiences they need to grow as leaders, and rise to their full potential in all areas of their lives. They are motivated to constantly improve themselves, adding value to themselves as they enhance their talents and abilities.

Identity leaders develop habits that help them improve their abilities, gain the experiences they need to grow as leaders, and rise to their full potential in all areas of their lives.

Identity Leaders Can Make Unpopular Decisions

Identity leaders have the courage to make unpopular decisions that are ultimately correct in terms of overall vision and goals. They speak their minds and are not swayed by popular opinion or peer pressure. That courage, by the way, is heightened by their self-understanding. They know what they believe, they know what they stand for and what their values are, and they are at peace with who they are. When you know who you are at your very core, then that core is much harder to shake.

Identity leaders are focused on staying the course and readjusting if that means it will hasten the realization of the vision or enhance its value, and they are ready to assert their reasons for decisions made along the way. And in emotionally charged situations, they are able to keep their emotions in check while clearly explaining their ideas and decisions.

> *The most difficult thing is the decision to act, the rest is merely tenacity.*
> —AMELIA EARHART

Identity Leaders Stay on Task

Identity leaders are focused in another way: they stay on task. It's a myth that multitaskers are better or more efficient workers; studies show they accomplish *less* than those who are more narrowly focused. When you are focused, you are better able to distinguish between relevant and irrelevant information. You are less likely to be distracted. You are better able to mentally file important information in your mind to be able to be quickly retrieved later. Your mind is more organized. You don't waste time skipping from one project or task to the next. You maintain continuity and flow in your work and your thought processes. You take the time to think deeply about a subject, develop your own ideas, go beneath the surface, and mine the gold that is below.

Identity Leaders Add Value to Their Organization

Identity leaders are highly valued for many other reasons that are all-important to companies. Among them are:

- **They drive performance.** Identity leaders understand the company's vision and goals and know what it will take to accomplish them. They know how to assess talent, put people in the places they will most likely succeed, pull a team together, and motivate people to work toward the common goal. And they know how to model the quality of work they need from others. They are out front leading that performance, and others are following their lead.
- **They cultivate collaboration.** Identity leaders see connections between people and departments and companies that will benefit all involved. They see the outcomes those collaborations can produce and can clearly present those outcomes to the key players to get them on board.
- **They see the potential in others.** Identity leaders see diamonds in the rough, and they also see new potential in key and experienced contributors. In an ever-evolving marketplace, this

ability to see potential in others is crucial to the growth and health of a company.

- **They support talent development.** Going hand in hand with seeing potential in others, they fully endorse and support the development of that potential. Identity leaders are highly motivated to spot, nurture, and develop talent, for the sake of both the company and the individual growth of the employee.
- **They forge relationships.** Identity leaders are like executive-level matchmakers. They see what they can offer to another group or organization and consider what that group can bring to the table so that both sides benefit. They shore up weaknesses through this forging of relationships and open up new opportunities in doing so.
- **They set the tone for company culture.** Identity leaders are in the position to set the tone for company culture, in part because people often look to natural leaders for their cues. Identity leaders are in tune with the company's values and culture and help to solidify that culture through their words and actions.
- **They encourage learning and innovation.** Identity leaders are voracious learners who value both learning and innovation. They recognize that innovation is the lifeblood of a company and create an environment where employees are motivated to learn and innovate.

Identity Leaders Are Responsible

Identity leadership is about being responsible to the people you are leading. That means you don't blame others when things go wrong. You don't blame circumstances that somehow sabotaged your project. You don't fall on your own sword and blame yourself in shame. You don't act out of an air of resigned obligation (this is one of the quickest ways to deflate a team's motivation). Instead, you take charge of and responsibility for your actions.

When you are an identity leader and intentionally act out of responsibility, then you develop an awareness of how you approach challenges. You catch yourself if you begin to blame others or circumstances or get down on yourself. You refuse to look at it from those angles. Instead, you look at the situation from a fresh set of perceptions and assumptions, knowing that you can and will find effective solutions.

And as you take responsibility as a leader, know this: those under you will become more responsible as well and will follow your lead. On the other hand, know that if you shirk responsibility, no individual or group is going to surpass your own level of responsibility. So, if you get in the habit of blaming others, either inside your company or outside of it, for your problems, know that the people under you will do the same. But if you tell your team, "Hey, this is our problem, let's figure out how to handle it," then they will take responsibility and pour their energies into solving the problem.

And as you take responsibility as a leader, know this: those under you will become more responsible as well and will follow your lead.

Identity Leaders Create the Outcomes They Want

I've talked about identity leadership in a business vein so far, but identity leadership is a 24/7 reality that touches every aspect of our lives—work, home, family, relationships, social, community, civic organizations, hobbies and extracurricular activities, passions, and pursuits of all shapes and sizes.

The common denominator in all these situations is that identity leaders know the outcome they are aiming for, they know themselves and their abilities and how those abilities pertain to their goals, and they have a plan for how to reach those goals. And they know how to lead and inspire others to reach those goals if it is a team and not an individual effort.

For example, let's say you are part of a social organization that wants to put on an event or raise funds for a worthy cause. But the organization, relying on its own resources, is going to fall short of the goal. You are aware of this, and you also are aware of other social or civic groups that your organization could partner with to reach the desired outcome. So you reach out to these other groups, get them on board, and your project becomes a big success.

Or let's say you have been working toward personal fitness goals for quite a while with no lasting success. Rather than continue to do the same thing over and over, you do deeper research on your own, maybe try different training programs or hire a personal trainer.

In other words, as an identity leader, you both perceive and do what it takes to reach the desired outcome, and you aren't hindered by roadblocks along the way. You negotiate around them until you reach your goal.

Identity Leaders Are Not Self-Centered

Sometimes when I talk about identity leadership, especially when I use the term *self-leadership*, people assume I am talking about people who are egotistical, self-centered narcissists. That couldn't be farther from the truth.

Identity leaders and self-leaders operate from a position of what is best for the organizational mission and goal. Their focus is on bringing people together in the right ways to accentuate strengths and accelerate growth. Identity leaders are like Broadway orchestra conductors, down in the pit, coordinating the efforts of all the musicians, who together produce what everyone came to hear: beautiful music. The audience did not come to watch the conductor wave his baton; they came to hear the amazing symphonic sound. The musicians are the center of attention, on stage; the conductor is in the pit, if not out of sight of the audience, at least out of mind. Yet the music does not get played without him.

Identity Leaders Aren't Afraid to Receive Criticism

Egotists and narcissists often get defensive when someone criticizes them, however valid that criticism might be. Identity leaders, on the other hand, are open to receiving criticism and complaints and can separate how those complaints were delivered from what those complaints stated. And if they delivered truth, then identity leaders learn from that truth, use it to grow, and are better off for it.

Here are three keys to embracing criticism and growing from it:

1. **Be confident in—and comfortable with—who you are.** With this mindset, you won't take criticism as an attack on your core identity. Two people can hear the same criticism and take it in very different ways. One might hear, *You are a massively flawed human being,* while the other might hear, *You made a mistake and here's how to fix it.*

2. **Use what is helpful and dump the rest.** Learn how to parse criticism that is on target and useful from criticism that is not helpful. View it all through the lens of the goal of the

project or work involved. Will it help you get there? Will it help you improve? If so, use it. If not, just thank the person and move on. You might get two minutes of criticism from someone in which all two minutes is useful. Or you might get two minutes in which about twenty seconds is useful—yet that twenty seconds might be extremely important. Learn to parse.

3. **When seeking feedback, ask specific questions.** General questions, such as "What did you think of our seminar?" are difficult for people to respond to very honestly or specifically. Instead, ask more specific questions, such as "In this part of our training seminar, should we have a group discussion or an individual activity?"

FIFTY-FOUR ATTRIBUTES OF IDENTITY LEADERS

Leaders rise to the fore for numerous reasons and in a variety of circumstances. Every leader is unique, but most share a significant number of attributes. Of course, not every leader is going to have every attribute on the following list, and some will be stronger in some areas than in others. But this is an aggregate compilation of the attributes of successful leaders that have arisen from numerous studies conducted on leadership.

As you read through this list, rate yourself on a scale of 1–5. If you score 140–190 points, you have average leadership skills. If you score 191–240 points, you have above-average skills. If you score above 240 points, your leadership skills are excellent.

(And if you don't want to tally your points, you can eyeball your marks to see where the majority of them fell.)

Effective leaders:	1 very poor	2 below average	3 average	4 above average	5 excellent
Are self-aware					
Are self-motivated					
Are honest and possess integrity					
Are authentic					
Are accountable and transparent					
Take responsibility					
Are always curious, always reading, and always learning					
Are resilient, persistent, and resourceful					
Are self-disciplined					
Are trustworthy and reliable					
Are passionate					
Are positive, confident, and courageous					
Have high social and emotional intelligence					
Are humble					
Respect others					
Set clear expectations					
Are fair					
Know how to inspire others					
Are good at delegating and empowering others					
See the potential in other people					

Help others succeed					
Lead in a way that is suited to their character, values, and goals					
Are committed and passionate					
Are good communicators					
Are assertive					
Are patient					
Know when to confront others appropriately and can do so					
Are empathetic					
Are good negotiators					
Are rewarders					
Develop a vision for the future					
Do not fear mistakes					
Are open-minded					
Are proactive					
Have good decision-making capabilities					
Invest in themselves and in others					
Are good at time management					
Work hard					
Network well					
Constantly work on their leadership and management skills					
Seek out advice					
Keep a sense of perspective					

Live in the present moment					
Are critical thinkers and synthesizers					
Are focused and engaged					
Adapt well to constant change					
Engage in a situation and see it through					
Leverage and transfer learning to other situations					
Are problem solvers and team builders					
Are relationship builders					
Are bold and innovative					
Know how to manage setbacks					
Are overcomers					
Are self-leaders first					

AN IDENTITY LEADER'S BEST FRIEND: A HIGH EQ

Emotional intelligence (commonly referred to as EQ) was a phrase first coined by psychologist and author Daniel Goleman back in the mid-1990s. In his research at nearly 200 global companies, Goleman found that the distinguishing characteristic among truly effective leaders was a high degree of emotional intelligence.[13]

In other words, all the education and experience in the world coupled with the most brilliant of minds does not make for a good leader.

When you bring that EQ factor into play, then that brilliance can shine through and your leadership potential will blossom.

An emotionally intelligent person is aware of his emotions, is able to express them and control them, and can handle relationships with wisdom and empathy. Emotionally intelligent people can harness and apply their emotions to tasks such as idea creation, decision making, and problem solving, and they have the ability to both sense others' emotional states and respond accordingly—for example, cheering them up, encouraging them, or calming them down.

Goleman found that the chief components of emotional intelligence—self-awareness, self-regulation, motivation, empathy, and social skill—directly impact measurable business results.

The so-called soft skills, the interpersonal skills that enable you to understand, relate to, and empathize with others, are every bit as important as the hard skills, those skills that are required to complete your job as required. In fact, it is the soft skills that will set you apart as a leader.

> The so-called soft skills, the interpersonal skills that enable you to understand, relate to, and empathize with others, are every bit as important as the hard skills, those skills that are required to complete your job as required.

NINE PRINCIPLES OF IDENTITY LEADERSHIP

If you want to activate the identity leader in you, take in and live out these nine principles that will help you achieve your vision and goals and help you fulfill your potential.

1. **Self-respect.** Respect who you are, your gifts and abilities, and the innate value that you have as a human being. There is literally no one in the world exactly like you. Treat yourself with the respect you deserve, and others will treat you with respect as well.

2. **Self-management.** Self-management has a great impact on your own behavior and well-being. Self-management begins with the self-talk that runs through our heads each day. The most successful people use positive, optimistic, and encouraging self-talk, which sways how they behave and feel and even what they attempt and do not attempt. Good self-managers challenge themselves to extend their boundaries, meet challenges, and grow.

3. **Self-development.** Every day we have opportunities to develop our character and our abilities. People who are intentional about developing themselves attain the greatest growth and are more likely to achieve their aims—in part because they shape their self-development around those aims.

4. **Self-responsibility.** Take responsibility for what you are answerable for and what you can control. Control your responses to those circumstances that are beyond your control. When you are self-responsible, you focus on the solution and move resourcefully toward your goals, no matter the circumstances. Self-responsibility moves us continually forward.

5. **Self-awareness.** When you are self-aware, you are conscious of your own character, feelings, motives, and desires. You also understand your strengths and weaknesses, the value you bring to a group, and your potential. People who are self-aware naturally attract others to them, because self-awareness says *I know who I am and what I can do.* That is attractive

precisely because so many people do not know who they are or what they can do. Self-aware people improve their performance, effectiveness, and success.

6. **Self-efficacy.** People with self-efficacy believe in their ability to perform to the levels they need to achieve goals. These beliefs determine how people think, feel, and motivate themselves to behave. Self-efficacy produces a resiliency in people, because they know they can overcome obstacles through planning, execution, effort, and perseverance. People with self-efficacy approach difficult tasks as challenges to be mastered rather than threats to be avoided. As Henry Ford said, "Whether you think that you can or you can't, you're usually right."

7. **Self-learning.** Identity leaders are continual learners throughout their lives. They are reading, observing, and asking questions; they are keeping up on the latest in their field; they are going to conferences, seminars, and workshops; they are learning from mentors, peers, and competitors; they are learning from their own experiences—and they are unafraid to try new experiences as they push the boundaries of their knowledge and skills.

8. **Self-motivation.** Self-motivators are people who are driven to accomplish goals regardless of external circumstances. They are committed to their goals and have a high level of initiative. They are ready to seize the opportunity to act toward those goals. They also tend to have high levels of optimism, which helps them push through barriers and obstacles along the way.

9. **Self-empowerment.** When you are self-empowered, you know who you are and what you are capable of, and this knowledge helps you set and reach goals that result in you

fulfilling your potential. Those who are self-empowered are able to take control of their circumstances to achieve their goals. They are aware of their strengths and weaknesses and thus better equipped to deal with problems, achieve goals, and take opportunities to enhance their personal and professional growth.

Take a moment to read back through that list, rating yourself in each principle using a scale of 1–5, with 1 being "extremely low" and 5 being "extremely high."

Don't be daunted if you don't rate yourself highly in every category. Becoming and being an identity leader is a process, an evolution, that takes place over time. Look for opportunities to build strengths where you feel you need to. Some of that improvement will come as you focus on that seventh principle, self-learning, which can help you in all the other categories.

THE IDENTITY LEADER ADVANTAGE

You've heard life described as a rat race. You wake up, you go to work, you work hard, you scrap for what you get, you compete against everyone and everything to do your job well, you're overworked, you're underpaid, and you're underemployed. You go home unhappy, you sleep, and you wake up and do it all over again.

That's a hard way to live.

As an identity leader, however, you can circumvent the rat race. As an identity leader, you have a lot of advantages that you can leverage in your career and your life.

I want to spell out some of those advantages. I've organized them in three categories: planning, performance, and personal development.

The Planning Advantage

Identity leaders have a great advantage in planning and organizing their lives around what's important to them. As an identity leader, you can:

1. **Make the most of your twenty-four hours.** Time is the great equalizer. We all have twenty-four hours to work with each day. Successful people don't have any more time than you do. But when you know who you are and what you're after, you spend your twenty-four hours carefully, thoughtfully, and wisely. You don't waste time, because you know that the choices you make with your twenty-four hours shape your life. You make choices that focus on your development and your goals. You figure out how to balance the priorities in your life and how to organize your life so that you move forward after your goals.

We all have twenty-four hours to work with each day. Successful people don't have any more time than you do. But when you know who you are and what you're after, you spend your twenty-four hours carefully, thoughtfully, and wisely.

2. **Use your whole brain to organize your life.** Many people get stuck using only one side of their brain (for a look at the right brain/left brain theory, see the sidebar "Right Brain, Left Brain, or Whole Brain"). Being an identity leader helps you to tap into unused portions of your brain to process

information from both creative and logical perspectives. The result is that you develop and sharpen your skills better. Your creative process strengthens your logical process, and vice versa.

3. **See what's possible.** When you know who you are and where you're going, you see potential ways for how you're going to get there. Possibilities begin to open up to you. What previously seemed fuzzy or daunting or unlikely now seems clear and achievable and worth going after. Identity leadership creates a new self-awareness about what is possible for you.

4. **Focus on what's important and relevant.** As an identity leader, you know what's important to you, and you eliminate distractions and behaviors that keep you from developing your full capabilities.

5. **Live from the internal, not the external.** In discovering your core identity, your focus shifts from the external to the internal. You aren't so swayed by external forces anymore—others' opinions of you, the circumstances of your life, the obstacles you might face—because you know internally who you are and what you are capable of overcoming and achieving.

6. **Know your core values.** Identity helps you explore and understand your core values. You learn what's truly important to you, what you believe in and what you believe about yourself, and these core values act as your rudder, guiding you into your future. It's on these core values that you base all your decisions and set all your goals.

7. **Gain a vision for your life.** When you know your core values, who you are and what you are about, you can gain a vision for your life. That vision springs from knowing your strengths and passions and from what really matters to you. And when you have such a vision, you place yourself ahead of the majority of people. Vision gives you purpose in your daily

living. Identity helps you achieve clarity and propels you forward both personally and professionally.

8. **Be consistent and focus on goals.** When you know who you are, you become much more consistent in your day-to-day living. That consistency stems from being sure of what you are after and from setting and focusing on short-term and long-term goals—the goals that, once achieved, will let the rest of the world know who you are, too. Identity leadership helps you develop habits that will increase your chance for success.

9. **Forge a career path and create a blueprint for success.** Identity leadership helps you forge a path for your career. This is the "how are you going to get there" part of "who are you, where are you going, and how are you going to get there." When you know those first two parts, the third part will fall into place. What was foggy becomes clear, and you can chart a path and a life that will be satisfying and fulfilling.

10. **Take control of your destiny and shape your future.** When you know what's relevant to your life, you can take control of your destiny. You find yourself in charge of your life and up to the task of shaping your future as you want it shaped. You are energized, because you not only know what you excel at and are passionate about but also know how to shape your life so that you play on those strengths and passions. As you build on your core values, you create a foundation for success. And as you become successful, you build on that success.

Control your own destiny or someone else will.

—JACK WELCH

Right Brain, Left Brain, or Whole Brain

The human brain is an amazing organ. It has about 100 billion neutrons and 100 trillion connections, and it is divided into two hemispheres. The left brain is more verbal, analytical, and orderly; the right brain is more visual, intuitive, and creative. From this understanding, the notion of being "right-brained" or "left-brained" came into vogue. But that notion has never been proven, and in a 2013 study from the University of Utah, brain scans on more than 1,000 people, which divided the brain into more than 7,000 regions, showed no evidence for "sidedness."[14] Personality traits, individual preferences, and learning styles aren't dependent on the idea that you might be right-brained or left-brained.

In fact, the two sides do not operate independently of each other, but in tandem with each other. For example, a left-brained person who is reading or writing (more left-brained functions) will use the right side to understand context and tone. The left side will do math equations, but the right side will assist by drawing comparisons and giving rough estimates.

What does that mean for us?

It means we should pay attention to developing the whole brain. We should play to our strengths while continuing to broaden our horizons on both sides of our brain. Then we will be able to function at our best.

The Performance Advantage

The first stage is planning; the second stage is performing. This third stage puts your plan into action. Going through the identity leadership process gives you significant advantages in this area, too. As an identity leader, you are able to:

1. **Achieve clarity and act with purpose.** When you know who you are, you know what you want. You are comfortable in your own skin. You don't feel the need to please others or try to be like someone else. You are fine with being yourself—and this frees you to see yourself, your life, and your possibilities with great clarity. In turn, that clarity helps you focus on your purpose and move toward it with confidence.

2. **Grow past your circumstances.** When you are secure in your identity, you can grow past your circumstances. You find that your old belief systems are outdated and no longer relevant to who you really are, just as your circumstances cannot keep the true you down. You now work through situations that you would have given up on before. You are no longer bound or penned in by unfortunate circumstances. You rise above them.

3. **Improve your time management skills.** Identity leadership helps you improve how you manage your time, because you know what you are after and you don't waste time on what's not relevant. You focus your day on what's important to you, based on your long-term and short-term goals.

4. **Create opportunities.** You find it easier to build relationship skills, improve your networking, and create more opportunities, because you know what you are after. When you know yourself, you are able to see opportunities you otherwise might have passed over. And the success you experience through the identity process paves the way for greater and deeper successes.

5. **Overcome obstacles.** Identity leadership is one of the biggest keys in overcoming obstacles. When you know who you

are and believe in yourself, you aren't deterred by obstacles in your way. You just figure a way around them.

6. **Improve your leadership skills.** As you go through the identity leadership process, you transform from a follower to a leader, because leaders are people who have no doubts about who they are and what they are capable of. Others naturally follow people like this, because they are drawn to people who have that self-understanding.

7. **See the world differently.** As an identity leader, you change the way you think and feel about yourself, and about your standing in the world. You become more confident, take responsibility for your own development, and change how you learn and how you process the information you come across, focusing on the information that is most important to your development. And the beautiful thing is that as you begin to see yourself and the world differently, the world follows suit. It sees you differently. Because you are different. You are the real you.

8. **Separate from the have-nots.** Remember that rat race I alluded to earlier? As an identity leader, you begin to separate yourself from the pack because you know what you're after— and this puts you ahead of most people. You have more opportunities to choose from, and you are among the early ones to choose.

9. **Create a competitive advantage.** Being an identity leader gives you a competitive advantage. When you have a foundation for your growth and development, when you can take information and knowledge and make it relevant to your life, you empower yourself to become an expert and to create value in your work. You set yourself up to become a producer instead of a consumer. And it's the producers, the leaders, that the world takes notice of.

10. **Maximize your potential.** Identity leadership helps you perform at your highest possible level, maximizing your potential in all that you undertake. You understand what motivates and drives you, and you know where you're going and how you're going to get there. You focus on the things that will help you continue to improve every day.

> Identity leadership helps you perform at your highest possible level, maximizing your potential in all that you undertake.

The Personal Development Advantage

This last section, on personal development, is just as important as the sections on planning and performance. Personal development is the foundation you build upon. Based on your personal development, you are better able to plan and perform. As an identity leader, you can:

1. **Care for and love yourself.** Self-love is a wholesome and healthy trait, not a narcissistic characteristic. Caring for and loving yourself means focusing on thoughts and actions that support your physical, psychological, and spiritual growth. When we operate in self-love, we don't feel the need to make excuses for our shortcomings; we accept who we are, wrinkles and all. And we are better able to stay focused on what is truly meaningful to us and what is aligned with our purpose and beliefs and values.

2. **Break a mindset of poverty.** People with poverty mindsets think this way: *Some people get all the breaks, but not me. I have nothing of value. I am destined to a life of poverty and drudgery*

and unhappiness, of seeing other people get what they want, but not having those same opportunities myself. Life isn't fair. I'm not saying those aren't valid feelings, but instead that identity leadership helps you break that mindset. You learn that the process for success is the same for everyone. There are countless stories of people who broke that poverty mindset because they knew who they were, and they did amazing things in their lives. They rose above their circumstances like an eagle lifting off the ground and flying high overhead. Identity leadership will help you fly like that eagle.

3. **Believe in yourself.** When you know yourself, you naturally believe in yourself. It's that simple. You know who you are, and belief follows knowledge. You are comfortable with and confident in who you are. And when you believe in yourself, you don't shrink from adversity. You don't let other people or circumstances confine you or dictate your life. You focus on who you are and what you can do, and you get it done. Belief in yourself is an invaluable—and necessary—tool for success.

4. **Shun external labels.** Labels are a huge problem and act as a trap for people who don't know who they are. But when you know your identity, you have the power to shun those labels and embrace the power to define yourself. You have the power to say, "No, I am not that type of person," "No, that is not who I am," and "No, I *can* do that."

5. **Remain motivated.** As an identity leader, motivation is easy for you. You know what you want, you pursue it, and you stay after it until you get it. People who don't know their identities would back off in the same situation. Identity leadership gives you a persevering power. It all hinges on having that clarity to know who you are, what you are after, why you are after it, and how you are going to get it.

6. **Build your brand.** Knowing your identity helps you to see your uniqueness. It's like focusing a lens before you snap a picture: what was fuzzy becomes distinct and clear. And when you are clear about yourself, you can begin to build your own brand and share your distinctness with those you meet. A brand says to the world, *This is who I am. This is what I can do. This is what you get when you work with me and know me.* Such a brand is a vital tool for you in both your professional life and your personal life.

7. **Build a foundation for continuous improvement.** Identity leadership is the key to improving yourself. The path to improving yourself is often slow and hard, but identity leaders have a foundation for continuous improvement. It frames and defines a process that helps you see clearly not only who you are but where you want to go and how you can get there.

8. **Create a path to freedom.** Identity leadership creates a path to freedom, because you know who you are and what you are worth. When you know who you are, you are free to be that person and explore your capabilities, passions, and dreams.

9. **Define and find success for yourself.** Identity leadership helps you define what success means to you. Success is different to different people. When you don't know who you are, your ideas of success are influenced by your friends and family and business associates, by the media, and by the culture you live in. You might be swayed to go this way one year and then that way another year, always chasing after a vague notion of success and never really finding it. But when you know who you are, you can clearly define what it means to you to live a successful life. You know in your heart what you are after, and living a life pursuing those passions and developing your abilities in those pursuits is at the root of your success.

10. **Build a life around what you enjoy and live life with purpose.** Through the identity leadership process, you create a life based on what motivates you, makes you happy, energizes you, and gives you purpose. You can build that life based on your passions and skills and strengths. You can dream big and go after it and not worry about what others say or think or shrink back from the obstacles you will come across. You have that solid identity foundation. Waves might crash against your boat, but they won't capsize it, and you'll navigate through or around any storm. Because, when you know your identity, you can't be stopped from fulfilling your purpose. You will live the most authentic life possible—the life you were meant to live.

Through the identity leadership process, you create a life based on what motivates you, makes you happy, energizes you, and gives you purpose. You can build that life based on your passions and skills and strengths.

Snapshot: The Identity Leader Advantage

This is the abbreviated list of advantages described in the text. As an identity leader, you can:

The Planning Advantage

1. Make the most of your twenty-four hours.
2. Use your *whole* brain to organize your life.
3. See what's possible.
4. Focus on what's important and relevant.

5. Live from the internal, not the external.
6. Know your core values.
7. Gain a vision for your life.
8. Be consistent and focus on goals.
9. Forge a career path and create a blueprint for success.
10. Take control of your destiny and shape your future.

The Performance Advantage

1. Achieve clarity and act with purpose.
2. Grow past your circumstances.
3. Improve your time management skills.
4. Create opportunities.
5. Overcome obstacles.
6. Improve your leadership skills.
7. See the world differently.
8. Separate from the have-nots.
9. Create a competitive advantage.
10. Maximize your potential.

The Personal Development Advantage

1. Care for and love yourself.
2. Break a mindset of poverty.
3. Believe in yourself.
4. Shun external labels.
5. Remain motivated.
6. Build your brand.
7. Build a foundation for continuous improvement.
8. Create a path to freedom.
9. Define and find success for yourself.
10. Build a life around what you enjoy and live life with purpose.

DEVELOPING IDENTITY LEADERSHIP SKILLS

By now I'm sure you see the importance of developing identity leadership skills. You see what having those skills can do in your life. Developing those skills plays a big role in answering the "How are you going to get there?" question. The truth is, you *aren't* going to get there without those skills intact and in play.

So, how do you go about developing these all-important skills? Here are eight keys to developing leadership skills.

1. **Develop your identity.** Just as you need to be able to lead yourself before you lead others, you need to know your identity—understand your passions, abilities, and gifts—before you can effectively develop as an identity leader. That identity gives you a foundation on which to build your identity leadership skills.

2. **Develop emotional intelligence.** Identity leaders are aware of, in control of, and able to express their emotions, and they manage relationships with empathy and understanding. Identity leaders understand their thought processes, behaviors, trigger points, strengths, and weaknesses, and they are able to inspire and influence those around them because of the emotional intelligence they possess.

3. **Be able to honestly assess yourself.** If you lie to yourself, make excuses for yourself, or view yourself in a false light—either too harshly or with too much sugarcoating—you are not going to be able to lead yourself or others, because you don't have an accurate picture of who you are.

4. **Be transparent and open in your relationships.** Just as you need to be open and honest with yourself, you need to be so with others. When you have a strong sense of identity, you

When you have a strong sense of identity, you are not afraid to be transparent, because you have nothing to hide, and what others think or say of you doesn't alter your understanding of who you are.

are not afraid to be transparent, because you have nothing to hide, and what others think or say of you doesn't alter your understanding of who you are. And the reality is that when you are transparent with others, sharing vulnerabilities, true feelings and thoughts, and not hiding weaknesses or flaws, people's opinions of you go higher, not lower. They will be drawn to you, want to learn from you, and have the self-confidence, like you do, to be comfortable in exposing their flaws and mistakes and show how they have learned from them.

5. **Be team- and goal-oriented.** Identity leadership is all about you developing your skills to their utmost and using them in pursuit of individual and team goals. Companies love identity leaders because they know they can count on such people to come through and lead others in achieving corporate goals.

6. **Be willing to take ownership.** The easy way out is to not take ownership of anything until you are sure that your endeavor is going to be recognized in a positive light and rewarded or lauded. Such a view is taken by people who jump on the bandwagon at the last moment—sort of like entering a marathon at mile 25 and running the last mile like you're a champion. Identity leaders are willing to go the entire distance and acknowledge ownership from the outset, when the

outcome is far from decided. They can do this because they are not relying on others to tell them who they are or how good they are. They can own their feelings, statements, and actions, because they are self-assured and will not be shaken regardless of outcome.

7. **Be able to adapt to change.** A trademark of identity leaders is the ability to size up situations and make changes when necessary. Identity leaders have the confidence to change a game plan in the middle of a game, because they have the emotional intelligence to see the need for change and trust their instincts and their abilities to be able to adapt on the fly. Those without such skills often stick to a bad game plan long after they realize things are not going well, simply because they are afraid to make a change. And they suffer the consequences for not following through on their instincts.

8. **Be authentic.** Perhaps more than anything else, identity leaders are authentic. They are who they are in both good times and bad. They don't change with the situation. You can count on identity leaders in all seasons of life, in all circumstances—in fact, you can count on them most when the chips are down, because you don't have to wonder about their true identities or what they are made of, because they have been transparent all along. Identity leaders are consistent, dependable, clear, honest, and genuine. What you see is what you get.

Six Ways to Hone Your Identity Leadership Skills

You can further develop any skill you have, no matter how good (or how weak) you are at it. That's why professional athletes, concert pianists, and all sorts of professionals practice and work at their skills every day. Here are six ways you can hone your self-leadership skills:

1. **Be more selfless.** This might sound counterintuitive when you are talking about building self-leadership skills, but the reality is that self-leaders are very attuned to the feelings and needs of others. As you develop your EQ, you are more aware of the needs and emotions of others and can use your abilities to appropriately interact with and potentially help them.

2. **Consider the areas where you are most reluctant to be honest with yourself and others and ask yourself why this is so.** Then make it your goal to be more transparent in these areas. Look for a specific person to be honest and transparent with in these areas.

3. **Care for yourself, maintaining a healthy body, mind, and spirit.** Far from being selfish, this allows you to most effectively care for and impact others.

4. **Read books, articles, and blogs on self-leadership.** Never stop learning. It's so vital to continuing to grow and improve.

5. **Identify and embrace your passions and focus more of your energy on them.** Drop activities or pursuits that take you away from your passions.

6. Accept yourself for who you are. Acknowledge your shortcomings and flaws, but also acknowledge your many gifts and abilities, and focus on those. Psalm 139 talks about how fearfully and wonderfully we are made: "For you formed my inward parts; you knitted me together in my mother's womb. I praise you, for I am fearfully and wonderfully made" (13–14a ESV). Recognize the glorious potential that is built into you. That is the core of your true identity, and identity leaders both grasp and operate under this reality.

IDENTITY LEADERSHIP KEYS

- Leadership is not devoid of stress. You need to learn how to manage stress in healthy ways. Also, work on enhancing your communication skills and give yourself time to grow into your leadership role.
- Identity leaders are able to make the unpopular decision. They add value to their organization by driving performance and bringing out the best in everyone. They are able to take criticism and grow from it, and they create the outcomes they want.
- Emotional intelligence is a key ingredient in leadership. A person with high EQ can express and control emotions, handle relationships well, and is skilled at idea creation, decision making, and problem solving.
- Nine principles of identity leadership include self-respect, self-management, self-development, self-responsibility, self-awareness, self-efficacy, self-learning, self-motivation, and self-empowerment.

- Eight keys to developing leadership skills are understanding your identity, developing your EQ, honestly assessing yourself, being transparent and open in relationships, being team- and goal-oriented, being willing to take ownership, adapting to change, and being authentic.

CHAPTER 7

Reaching Your Full Potential as a Leader

The biggest opportunity today—and it is wide open—is in leadership.

Even after I earned a master's degree in education, I wasn't sure what I wanted to do. I couldn't answer those three questions I posed earlier, the three critical questions we all have to answer: *Who am I? Where am I going? How am I going to get there?*

I ended up working at a succession of jobs that were not very satisfying or fulfilling. In the meantime, I was around a lot of people who were happy in their work, focused on their development, and independent in their thinking. I realized I was missing the boat. I saw, quite starkly, the difference between people who have a purpose and people who don't. So, I set about trying to discover my purpose, trying to find out what I truly cared about and how I could structure my life around that passion.

But that is much easier said than done. It can take a long time for people to do that. It did for me.

This was in the mid-1980s, in my early years of my relationship with Oprah. She was happy, she loved her life, and she was successful. I wanted to find that same happiness and success in my career. At first, I thought it might be in the clothing business. So, I worked in a clothing store, but I found I didn't like that. What I did like was being around people, relating to people. I'm a people person. So, I found work in public relations, marketing, and advertising for a while. The people part of that work I enjoyed, but the technical side, not so much.

All the while, going through this process, I was learning about myself. I was learning what really mattered to me, what I liked to do, what I didn't like to do, and what my strengths and weaknesses were. Slowly but surely, I was refining my search in understanding my core identity and my purpose.

As I continued, I realized that both the search for identity and purpose and the process I was going through were not unique to me. It was what we all go through, or need to go through. And this drive to communicate this with others—being the people person that I am, and truly wanting to help others reach their potential—began to grow in me.

What I was going through is the process of self-actualization. I was discovering my core purpose and passion, and I decided—no, I *knew*—I needed to share what I was learning with others. *That* was what I was passionate about: helping other people self-actualize, showing them how to maximize their potential as human beings and supporting them in their dreams and aspirations.

It was a years-long process, but I finally could answer those three questions: *Who am I? Where am I going? How am I going to get there?*

From that self-understanding, my book, *You Can Make It Happen: A Nine-Step Plan for Success*, was born, my business was established, and, more importantly, the work of my hands—what I was put here on this earth to do—was clarified.

THE POWER OF SELF-ACTUALIZATION

American psychologist Abraham Maslow, best known for his hierarchy of needs theory and renowned for his work in human motivation and developmental psychology, once said, "A musician must make music, an artist must paint, a poet must write, if he is to be ultimately at peace with himself."[15]

In other words, we are born with innate desires and abilities that bring us fulfillment as we develop them. That is why musicians and artists and poets are at peace when they are making music, painting, and writing. That is why a doctor feels right when she is diagnosing or treating an illness or disease, why an auto mechanic is in a groove when he is fixing a car, why a guidance counselor loves it when she is helping a student. It is what they were born to do, it is what they do well, and it is what brings them joy. It is, as Maslow would say, what they need to do. That is how he described self-actualization:

What a man can be, he must be. This need we call self-actualization.[16]

Further, it is where they belong. It is where we all belong: on the road to self-actualization. Because self-actualization is not a destination; it is a journey. It is an ongoing process of developing and using our abilities. It is stoking that fire inside us that keeps us moving toward our potential, that keeps us alert to the possibilities around us that will help us reach our promise. It is finding ways to expand our capabilities, nurture them, strengthen them, embrace them, grow them, use them, and unleash them upon the world.

Thomas Edison, the holder of more than 1,000 patents for inventions, said this about potential: "If we did all the things we were capable of, we would literally astound ourselves." People who are far along the road of self-actualization not only astound themselves; they astound those around them. They astound the world they live in, because they achieve great things and they lead in ways that are uncommon.

When you are self-actualized, the world opens up to you as it never has before. And it is the best identity leaders who are farthest along the road to self-actualization.

When you are self-actualized, the world opens up to you as it never has before. And it is the best identity leaders who are farthest along the road to self-actualization.

In the end, it is important to remember that we cannot become what we need to be by remaining what we are.

—MAX DE PREE

DEFINING SELF-ACTUALIZATION

Self-actualization is a fancy term for realizing or fulfilling your potential. It's an innate drive that we all have. Maslow, in defining the term, said that people who are self-actualizers:

- Are in the ongoing process of developing their potential, capacity, and talent
- Are moving toward fulfilling their personal mission or destiny
- Have a fuller knowledge of and acceptance of their intrinsic nature
- Are moving toward unity or integration within their life

Self-Actualization and the Self-Fulfilling Prophecy

A self-fulfilling prophecy is a prediction that comes true either directly or indirectly because of the prophecy itself. The man who coined this phrase, sociologist Robert Merton, defined a self-fulfilling prophecy as an initially false definition of a situation that evokes a behavior that makes the false conception come true.

The concept of self-actualization, then, is central to the theme of this book: developing your whole self and your full potential. Those are the hallmarks of an identity leader.

MASLOW'S HIERARCHY OF NEEDS

In 1943, Abraham Maslow published a paper called "A Theory of Human Motivation" in *Psychological Review*. That paper detailed his hierarchy of needs (commonly represented in a pyramid, which, ironically, he neither mentioned nor used in his work talking about needs). He categorized five types of needs, in the order in which they are most met: physiological, safety, love and belonging, esteem, and self-actualization.

For the sake of illustration, he wrote that a person might have these percentages of his needs met: 85 percent of his physiological needs, 70 percent of his safety needs, 50 percent of his love needs, 40 percent of his self-esteem needs, and 10 percent of his self-actualization needs. (That's why the physiological needs are at the base of the pyramid that someone else constructed; those needs are met more than the others.)

Maslow further broke down the five needs into two categories: basic needs (physiological and safety) and growth needs (love, esteem,

Pyramid showing Maslow's hierarchy of needs

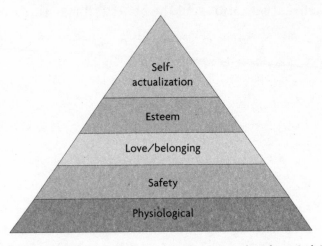

Credit: Retrieved from Wikimedia Commons: https://commons.wikimedia.org/wiki/File:MaslowsHierarchyOfNeeds.svg

and self-actualization). It is only when you have your basic needs met, he said, that you can move on and fulfill your growth needs.

Fulfilling needs at each level is a prerequisite for moving to the next level. And that's why it's so rare that a person's self-actualization needs are met; she doesn't have the time at that level, because her needs have not yet been met at the other levels.

TWELVE CHARACTERISTICS OF SELF-ACTUALIZED PEOPLE

In Maslow's studies on self-actualization—and he used Albert Einstein, Harriet Tubman, Abraham Lincoln, Eleanor Roosevelt, Jane Addams, Thomas Jefferson, and many others as models—he found these common traits:[17]

1. **They embrace the unknown.** They are not threatened by it; indeed, they are often intrigued by the unknown.

2. **They know and accept themselves.** They know their strengths and accept their weaknesses.

3. **They know it's about the journey, not the destination.** They enjoy the journey for its own sake.

4. **They tend to be unconventional, but they don't press unimportant issues.** They don't get hung up in arguments or combat rituals of convention if no great issues are at stake. They can let all that go.

5. **They are focused on growth.** They do not focus on their basic needs, but on personal growth and development.

6. **They have purpose.** They are focused on a mission, on something larger than themselves. Their purpose is nonpersonal, unselfish, and tied to the greater good of mankind.

7. **They aren't troubled by the small things.** They remain focused on the bigger picture, on their purpose.

8. **They are grateful.** They are able to appreciate their blessings and the good things in life and maintain a wonder about the world and its possibilities.

9. **They have deep relationships.** They tend to have more profound interpersonal relations than others do. They also feel a deeper empathy for the human race, and act with benevolence and affection toward people.

10. **They are humble.** They aren't puffed up with pride. They look to learn from other people and are aware they have much to learn.

11. **They make their own decisions.** They are not swayed by the culture, popular opinion, or anything else. They make up their own minds, knowing they are responsible for their own destinies.

12. **They are not perfect.** They are, after all, human! They have faults and shortcomings and can have irritating qualities as well.

That last trait is important to remember, because the first eleven traits can make self-actualized people seem very close to perfect— almost a race of superhumans. And this is not the case. They merely are people who are advanced along the journey of getting the most out of their capabilities, understanding their purpose, and giving back to society as they live that purpose out.

> *A winner is a dreamer who never gives up.*
> —NELSON MANDELA

THE SELF-ACTUALIZED LEADER

As you move along on your journey of self-actualization, you become a better leader. After reading about the power of self-actualization and characteristics of self-actualized people, that should be easy to understand.

Self-actualized leaders are in it for the greater good. They are perceptive about the people below them and insightful about helping them grow. They aren't held back by labels, others' opinions, fears, failure, or anything else. They have a healthy attitude about themselves, others, and their place in the world.

They keep developing their abilities; they keep moving toward their fullest potential, regardless of their position in life or current circumstances. And as they do, they enhance their leadership skills and rise up in their organization because of the greater value they are bringing to it.

Identity leaders keep developing their abilities; they keep moving toward their fullest potential, regardless of their position in life or current circumstances. And

as they do, they enhance their leadership skills and rise up in their organization because of the greater value they are bringing to it.

Martin Luther King Jr.: A Self-Actualized Man

Martin Luther King Jr. is a great example of a self-actualized man. Perhaps the greatest civil rights leader this country has ever known, King embodied so many of the characteristics of a self-actualized person. He had a purpose, and that purpose was tied to the greater good of mankind. He embraced the unknown. He was not swayed by culture and popular opinion. He was humble. He moved relentlessly toward his destiny. He was creatively expressive. He indeed had a dream, and that dream was bigger than himself.

He organized bus boycotts and nonviolent protests. He helped organize the 1963 March on Washington, where he delivered his famous "I Have a Dream" speech. He was awarded the Nobel Peace Prize in 1964, and after he was assassinated in 1968, he was posthumously awarded the Presidential Medal of Freedom and the Congressional Gold Medal.

King operated at the self-actualization level that Maslow described. It would be literally impossible for a person to accomplish what he accomplished and live the life he lived without being self-actualized. King was living his life to the fullest, and that he was gunned down in the prime of his life does not diminish what he achieved or how he achieved it.

Victims make excuses. Leaders deliver results.

—ROBIN SHARMA

MOVING TOWARD SELF-ACTUALIZATION

Maslow said that human beings are hardwired to self-actualize. That's important to understand. Self-actualization isn't for some superset of elite leaders. It's for everyone. Maslow said, "I think of the self-actualizing man not as an ordinary man with something added, but rather as the ordinary man with nothing taken away."[18]

So, as we were naturally created, we by default move toward self-actualization. That's the good news. And the even better news is that later in this book I will guide you through that entire process of self-actualization when I take you through my Nine-Step Success Process. Through that process, you will construct your own identity leadership plan.

But before you get there, I want to share a few thoughts with you regarding some of the keys to moving toward self-actualization. Here are eight keys to developing your full potential:

1. **Measure your progress against yourself, not others.** Self-actualization, as its name implies, has nothing to do with other people. It's all about your development. Whether you measure higher or lower than others is meaningless. It's where you are on the spectrum of developing your own abilities and potential that matters.

2. **Remember that you are in control of your development.** Don't expect others to be in charge of your development. Be proactive. Take control of your own destiny. Certainly enlist others along the way—we'll talk more about that in the final chapter—but know that you are responsible for developing fully as an identity leader by becoming a self-actualized person.

3. **Keep growing.** The best identity leaders literally never stop learning and growing. And you really need to keep growing, because our world is changing ever faster. Identity leaders understand that

the journey is never over, and the journey—not the destination—
is what it's all about. The best leaders are the best learners.

4. **Live in the moment.** Yes, leaders have to look to the future,
but they live in the present. Sometimes great opportunities
come our way and we miss them because we are dwelling on
a past mistake or worrying about or plotting out the future.
Keep your eyes open. Absorb what is going on around you.
Let down your defenses, your stances, your posturing. You
might be surprised at what you discover right in front of you.

5. **Be aware of the choices in front of you.** Maslow said that
all throughout the day we make choices—either toward self-
actualization or retreating toward safety, toward the known,
away from fear. Make choices that feed into your growth
rather than stunt it.

6. **Be honest with yourself and others.** There's no need to play
games or try to impress people that you're someone you're not.
The better you know yourself, the more comfortable you are
in your own skin, the easier it is to show your true self, to be
your true self, and to not feel you have to apologize for or
defend your thoughts and feelings.

7. **Set up for peak experiences.** These peak experiences can
accelerate your growth and development, and they come about
when you open up to the situations where your greatest poten-
tials are. So, if you are a writer, you set up for peak experiences
by attending conferences where you can meet the types of writ-
ers, agents, and editors who can help you grow; by networking
with the same; by being active in professional writing organizations; and so on. Place yourself in the best position to grow.

8. **Keep moving toward your destiny.** When you do all the
other things on this list—when you focus on your own
progress and development, when you are continually learning, when you are open to the opportunities in the present,

when you make daily choices that move you toward self-actualization, when you are comfortable with and honest with yourself, and when you experience peaks—you will be moving toward your destiny. And when you are moving toward your destiny, you are becoming more and more self-actualized, and you are growing as an identity leader.

Throughout our day we make choices—either toward self-actualization or retreating toward safety, toward the known, away from fear. Make choices that feed into your growth rather than stunt it.

The Relationship between Fear and Potential

Some people have the misconception that great leaders operate outside the boundaries of fear, that fear somehow cannot touch them. It logically follows that if they experience fear, they must not be cut out to be a leader.

This simply isn't true. Leaders experience fear; after all, they're human, right? But great leaders don't let fear stop them from doing what they are called to do.

Leaders are quite often in a place to feel fear or trepidation, because they are forever learning, extending their boundaries, solving problems, exploring, and taking risks. Unknowns proliferate in these circumstances. Leaders simply understand when to push through and navigate through their fear. Because, quite often, on the other side of that fear is more growth and development.

Don't let fear stop you from reaching your full potential.

TAPPING INTO YOUR FULL POTENTIAL

Self-actualization is the journey you undertake to tap into your full potential. It's about continual learning and growth, extending boundaries, acquiring new skills and enhancing old ones, and growing in your leadership abilities.

To lead effectively—first yourself, then others—you have to be moving forever toward your full potential. It's a moving target, because as you grow and develop your skills, your potential increases. And as your potential increases, your identity leadership skills multiply. It's an invigorating process that keeps life interesting and full and brings you satisfaction as you enjoy doing what you do best and naturally increase your sphere of influence as your skills increase.

So keep tapping, keep going down that road of self-actualization, because it helps you live your life to the fullest, and it will hone the identity leadership skills you need to be successful in your professional and personal life.

IDENTITY LEADERSHIP KEYS

- Self-actualization is not a destination; it is a journey. It is an ongoing process of developing and using our abilities. It is stoking that fire inside us that keeps us moving toward our potential and keeps us alert to the possibilities around us that will help us reach our promise. It is finding ways to expand our capabilities, nurture them, strengthen them, embrace them, grow them, use them, and unleash them upon the world.

- *Self-actualization* is a fancy term for realizing or fulfilling your potential. It's an innate drive that we all have. The concept of self-actualization, then, is central to the theme of this book: developing your whole self and your full potential. Those are the hallmarks of an identity leader.

- If you focus on self-actualization, on understanding and reaching your potential and developing your abilities, all the needs in Maslow's Hierarchy of Needs will be met: physiological, safety, love, and esteem.

- Self-actualized leaders make the best leaders for many reasons: they aren't held back by labels, they keep developing their abilities, they help others grow, and they have a healthy attitude about themselves and their place in the world.

- Self-actualization is directly related to identity leadership because it is the journey you undertake to tap into your full potential.

CHAPTER 8

The Nine-Step Story

Take the small steps and your momentum will build.

I came out with the book *You Can Make It Happen: A Nine-Step Plan for Success* in 1997. A lot of water has passed under the bridge since then. But those steps have stood the test of time. They are as strong and relevant today as they were twenty-some years ago. That book became a *New York Times* bestseller, as did a sequel geared toward teens called *Teens Can Make It Happen*. The same steps that apply to adults apply to teens. That's part of the beauty and strength of the steps.

When you look at the steps (see the sidebar, "The Nine Steps"), you see a pattern to them, an order in how they are shaped. There is a logical flow to them and a connection among them. They function like a Slinky, that flexible toy spring that can walk down steps. One step follows the other, and so on, until you complete all the steps. The nine steps have a clarity and a simplicity to them that makes people say, "Yeah! That makes sense!"

That logical flow and simplicity might lead people to believe that it all fell into place easily for me, that it just came to me one inspired evening. That would have been nice, but that's not how it happened.

The reality is that those steps came together for me slowly and sometimes painfully. They weren't the result of momentary inspiration but of months and years of trying to make a name for myself, trying to understand my own identity and purpose, trying to overcome some major roadblocks along the way.

Building those nine steps was a process and a journey. Let me share just a bit of that journey with you.

The Nine Steps

1. **Check your ID.** Before deciding what to do in life, you must first understand who you are, what influences your life, and why you think and act the way you do.

2. **Create your vision.** Your vision is your life's destination. A well-defined vision helps you define meaningful and achievable goals. Design a powerful future based on possibility rather than on circumstances.

3. **Develop your travel plan.** If you are to fulfill your vision for a better life, you must create a plan of action. By working toward goals through a solid plan of action based on your identity, you learn to assert power over your life.

4. **Master the rules of the road.** Guidelines keep you on track as you engage in the pursuit of a better life. Learn to use the positive power of honesty, hard work, determination, and other solid values to guide you as you journey toward your dreams.

5. **Step into the outer limits.** To grow, you have to leave your comfort zone, confront fears, and take risks. Learn how to

overcome fear and step outside of what has become comfortable and familiar to you.

6. **Pilot the seasons of change.** If you keep doing what you have always done, you will keep getting the same results. Learn how to create change and, even more importantly, how to manage your responses to change.

7. **Build your dream team.** No one makes it alone. Learn how to build supportive relationships that help you work toward your goals. You learn the value of trust and the importance of being trustworthy.

8. **Win by a decision.** Who you are in this world is largely the result of the decisions you have made in the past. By learning how to make the right choices for your future, you set yourself up for success.

9. **Commit to your vision.** When you consistently devote your time and energy to the pursuit of your goals and vision, you discover that commitment is a nonnegotiable trait that, when renewed daily, propels you toward your dream.

I am not a product of my circumstances. I am a product of my decisions.

—STEPHEN R. COVEY

THE NINE-STEP JOURNEY

Lao Tzu, the great Chinese philosopher, said that a journey of a thousand miles begins with one step. My own journey into developing the process that eventually became known as the Nine-Step Success Process began with my desire to brand my sports marketing business to distinguish it from others in a crowded marketplace. Sports marketing was and is a huge industry. In 2017, annual company spending for sports advertising in the US was nearly $38 billion. The global sports market is estimated to be worth between $600 billion and $700 billion a year. Its growth outpaces the GDP growth of most countries. So you can see the need for branding, for clearly identifying who you are and what you have to offer.

Before I started my own sports marketing business, I worked for B&C Associates, a global business management consulting firm in North Carolina. Bob Brown, the *B* of B&C and the founder of the company, is a great man and tremendous leader. I had the privilege of being mentored by Bob and learned so much from him about how to operate in business, how to build relationships, how to make wise decisions, how to manage my time and talents, how to cast vision… the list could go on and on.

The Importance of Brand

One of the lessons Bob taught me was the importance of a brand. B&C has a strong reputation around the world in business management consulting; they are trusted and respected, and you know what to expect from them as a company. You know what they value, how they will treat you, and what they can do for you. You know the value they are going to bring to the table.

And that's exactly what I wanted for myself and my new sports marketing company. I wanted clients to know who I was, what they could expect from me, and what my company could do for them. So, as I began to think about building my own brand, I did a lot of research. I studied IMG, the global sports, events, and talent management company. IMG is a hugely successful company, founded by Mark McCormack, whom I knew (he has since passed away). IMG has a strong and distinctive brand, and while my brand would be different, I could certainly learn a lot from the company. I also studied some other successful organizations, examining their approach to being successful in the marketplace and determining what their brand was and, to the extent that I could, how they had built it.

Two Aha Moments

What I learned in my studies was this: all these successful companies had systems in place that maximized their employees'—and the company's—potential. Each system was built around a core, the primary strength or purpose of that company. Everything flowed out from that core, and everything connected to that core.

Just as importantly, I also discovered that it didn't matter if it was a global company or a regional or local company. It could have 50,000 employees or it could have five employees. If it was successful, if it had a distinctive brand, a business identity that was its calling card in the marketplace, then it had systems in place built around that core.

That was one aha moment for me, realizing that you didn't have to be a multinational corporation to attain success or to have a strong brand. It's not the size of the company that matters. It's the impact of the company. And a small company can have great impact. In fact, small businesses account for nearly three-quarters of all jobs in the US. And they produce thirteen times more patents than larger firms. That's because there are more than 25 million small businesses in America.

But I had another even more important aha moment as I continued to learn about how I could brand my company and successfully grow it. I realized that the system approach I was discovering in successful large businesses could be applied to individuals as well as small businesses.

I realized that the system approach I was discovering in successful large businesses could be applied to individuals as well as small businesses.

In other words, it wasn't just a business thing. It was a *life* thing—one that encompassed your life whether at work or play, at the community or family level, your hobbies and passions. This approach—which eventually became shaped into the nine steps—covered your coming and going, your waking and sleeping, your today and tomorrow. It covered *everything*.

Because just as businesses build brands, so do people.

Stephen Covey's Influence

I met Stephen Covey, the author of the highly popular *The 7 Habits of Highly Effective People*, at a conference in the late 1980s. He invited me to a seminar he was giving in the Sundance Resort near Provo, Utah. Stephen was a brilliant man and a great speaker, educator, and businessman. He was process oriented, and in this seminar he presented principles on organizational development. I found his content to be fascinating, because it was exactly what I needed.

Stephen and I struck up a friendship, and he became a mentor of mine. When I was out West, I would spend some time with him, and when he was in Chicago, we would get together as well.

Stephen was an inspiration to me. He encouraged me and was a role model for me, and he still holds a special place in my heart. I could always talk to him about this kind of work. In my estimation, he was the best in the industry. There was no one better when it comes to the development of human potential. I will always be grateful to Stephen for pushing me farther along on my journey to discover the process that would work for me— the process that I am sharing in this book.

MOTIVATED TO CHANGE

I continued working on these ideas as I explored what it meant for me to create a system or process that would work for my business and for me. I knew I was onto something, but it took me a while to see exactly what it was. However, I was motivated on multiple levels to go through this process, knowing that I could use it to guide my career and help establish my business.

When we're comfortable in life, we aren't motivated to change. We're fine with the status quo. Why fix what's not broken, right? But when we experience discomfort, when things in our life are not right, when we are being held back from our goals, when we're frustrated and not living the life we want to live, then we have the motivation to change.

Labeled by Skin and Circumstances

Back in the 1980s, when I was mulling all this over and starting new businesses and foundations, I wanted to change. Quite frankly, I was tired of being labeled. Race is and always has been a huge issue in America; it's both terrible and ridiculous that people can be marginalized based on the color of their skin.

I have two brothers who are mentally disabled. In a small town, you are known not only for who you are, but for who your family is. I struggled with self-esteem and identity issues from very early on in life. Self-esteem and identity are gigantic issues for a lot of people—for many, they are insurmountable. Some give up trying, because those issues are too daunting.

Labeled by Relationship

Then, in 1986, I began a relationship with Oprah, who would become one of the most famous people in the world. I have always been a private person. I love people. I love engaging with them, and I love seeing the potential in them and helping them see how to draw it out of themselves. But I don't love my personal life being paraded in front of the world. But that's how tabloids make their money, and so for decades, my relationship with Oprah has been bandied about in the press, sensationalized and distorted, all for the purpose of moving papers.

So here I was, searching for my own identity, trying to get my business and career established, and all of a sudden my picture is on the front pages of the tabloids in the supermarket newsstands. And the stories inside those papers were defining who I was to the world. I already had my own pain to heal before any of that happened; that just added fuel to the fire.

It also added tension to the process. It made me want to figure things out quicker, because I hated the labels and lies that the media was using to present me to the world. I knew I had to define myself, and I doubled down in my efforts to do so.

Two Keys: Persistence and Optimism

I was helped greatly by two aspects of my character: I am not a quitter, and I am a glass-half-full person. When I was an athlete all the way through college and beyond, I was very motivated by goals and motivated to show people who didn't believe in me what I could do. I still have a dogged determination to achieve the goals that I set for myself. I relentlessly pursue them, regardless of how difficult they are. The more difficult they are, the sweeter it is when I do attain them.

My positive outlook helped me immensely through what otherwise could have been some very dark times. While I did struggle with self-esteem when I was younger, I always deep down believed in myself. I always knew I was worth something, just as all humans are worth something. Having a positive outlook helped me believe in myself, believe in better things ahead, believe that I would find a way to those better things ahead. I had this voice inside me saying *I can do it. I can find a way to do this.*

Thinking you can do it is the first and most critical step in doing it. The difference between a positive and negative outlook is the difference between a penthouse and a prison, a prince and a pauper, a risk taker and a couch potato, a champion and a nonparticipant—which is worse than a loser, because the loser at least tried.

The difference between a positive and negative outlook is the difference between a penthouse and a prison, a prince and a pauper, a risk taker and a couch potato, a champion and a nonparticipant— which is worse than a loser, because the loser at least participated.

SLOWLY COMING INTO SHAPE

The nine steps formed over time as I continued to work through the process that was relevant to my business growth and personal growth. Looking back, I liken the process to sculpting. I was taking the core material that would help me build a brand not only for my business but also for myself as a person, and I was shaping it, refining it, and honing it. I was working with solid principles that promoted growth, and I was making them mine.

This process took a few years and continued to be fine-tuned for several more after that. Ever so slowly, the steps became clearer and more well defined, and they became very energizing to me, because I realized I was onto something. When I dusted them all off, I saw I had nine principles, nine steps in place, and as I looked closely at them, I realized that there was a logical flow and an interconnection between them, that one built upon the other, just as steps in a staircase do. That's how they came to be called the nine steps. And when you ascend those steps, you find yourself in a place where you not only have greater vision of the landscape and possibilities before you, but you also have a greater understanding of how to conquer that landscape and realize those possibilities because you understand the principles behind those steps, you have worked through them, and you have become a self-actualized identity leader.

People who don't take risks generally make about two big mistakes a year. People who do take risks generally make about two big mistakes a year.

—PETER F. DRUCKER

Seeing the Big Picture Come Together

You've heard the saying "I can't see the forest for the trees." That happens when you are so focused on the details that you can't see the big picture. When you immerse yourself in a big process or complex work, that often happens. And then you take a brief break, step back, and all of a sudden you can see the big picture.

That happened to me in working through the nine-step process. I was so immersed in the details of identity and vision and planning and all the other steps that I didn't realize, for quite some time, what the bigger picture was.

And then I stepped back and saw that all of these steps led to a specific destination: self-actualization. Each of the steps on its own was powerful and important, but, put together, I saw that you could truly shape your own future, create your own life, and actualize your potential.

I saw the power of these steps packaged together: They dealt with education; internal, social, emotional, and intellectual issues; relationships; spirituality; work; health; and goals and aspirations—in short, they dealt with all aspects of your life. And they dealt with those aspects in ways to make your life better, to give you actionable steps to take toward understanding and fulfilling your potential.

That realization gave me even greater energy to work through the steps, knowing the outcome—seeing the value of that forest that was made up of those trees I was working on.

THE NINE STEPS WORK AT BOTH CORPORATE AND INDIVIDUAL LEVELS

The nine steps are equally relevant to individual growth. The steps helped me forge my identity. They helped me keep my sanity as the media tried to tell the world who I was. The media doesn't know who I am. *I* know who I am, and by going through the nine steps I built my company, created a foundation, and established both a corporate brand and a personal brand. Labels no longer stick to me. I had many labels attached to me throughout my life, labels that were painful and debilitating, but they all slide harmlessly off me now.

That's because the nine steps work. They are forged from solid life principles, but principles in and of themselves usually don't change us. What is required for change is putting those principles into practice. In working through the nine steps for myself, I created a process that takes the theory behind the principles and makes them practical. That's another reason why I call them steps. The word *steps* denotes activity and movement. Reading about sound theory can change your thinking. Putting that sound theory into practice can change your life.

THE CORNERSTONE STEP: IDENTITY

Identity is the cornerstone of the nine steps. It is the foundation upon which the other eight steps are built. If you don't know who you are, if you don't know your passions and talents, if you don't know what makes you tick at your very core, then you can't move forward with the other steps. Philosophers have been asking those questions for millennia: *Who am I? What is my purpose? Why am I here?*

The nine steps help you answer those questions and many others, but it all necessarily hinges on that *Who am I?* question. When you can answer that—and I will show you how to do so in the next chapter—you unlock the door to tapping into your full potential, identifying and realizing your dreams and ambitions, and becoming the identity leader you were meant to be.

THE LIFE-CHANGING POWER OF THE NINE STEPS

The nine steps have a singular focus: to help you self-actualize and be the best version of yourself that you can be. People who do this find themselves in places of leadership. You will find as you go through the identity leadership process that others will be attracted to you, because they want what you have. People innately understand when they are in the presence of a self-actualized person, because that person exudes a confidence and a humility and a strength of vision about themselves; passion and purpose seem to ooze from their pores.

Our mantra in the Stedman Graham Identity Leadership program is *Purpose, passion, and performance.* Going through the identity leadership process, you will develop greater insight and understanding of your purpose and your passion, and you will elevate your performance. It's all part of "Who am I? Where am I going? How am I going to get there?" Those questions are answered through the identity leadership process.

This process was a long time in the making, but the struggles and effort were entirely worth it. I realized that what I built for myself had great value and relevance for the world. I have taught the nine steps in China, South Africa, Rwanda, Canada, and the Netherlands. I have taught it to the military, corporate leaders, business executives at all levels, and junior high and high school and college students. I have taught it to people living in poverty and people living in comfort.

Why? Because the nine steps work. They are highly practical. They are eye-opening and inspiring. They are relevant to every human being who has breath. They are life changing.

The nine steps work. They are highly practical. They are eye-opening and inspiring. They are relevant to every human being who has breath. They are life changing.

Here's how they change your life. First, they change you on the inside. They crystalize your understanding of yourself, and they help you identify passions and dreams and create a vision for yourself. They motivate and energize you and help you form a plan for your life that accentuates your talents and your passions. As you realize your vision, your external world changes. From the subtle to the obvious, things change: how you present yourself to others, what you aim for, how you pursue it, the circles you run in, the passions you pursue, the habits you drop. You are more focused on what is meaningful to you, and you fashion your life around that. You realize what has been holding you back, and you let those things go. You make sacrifices that are in line with your vision. Your life changes—for the better. And you keep moving forward through the process, always growing, always learning.

And one day you look back and you realize how far you have come on your journey. You are amazed, because you took that journey one step at a time—but in this process, none of those steps are wasted, wandering, or off your path. You remember what Lao Tzu said about how a journey of a thousand miles starts. And you realize it's true.

If you knew how much work went into it, you wouldn't call it genius.

—MICHELANGELO

A Sampling of Nine-Step Case Studies

I began my work in the Netherlands in 2007, working with the Symposium Circustheater in the Hague, the US military community in Holland, and with numerous other organizations, foundations, schools, and companies.

I was also honored to conduct a nine-step seminar for about 4,000 refugees and immigrants in Amsterdam. The government was trying to assimilate them into their society, and the immigrants were sorely in need of the nine-step process because they were in a new land, experiencing a new culture, without a strong belief system about who they were. They had just come from Syria or an African country, parents with three or four or five kids, and they had given up everything to find freedom and a new life. You can imagine how inadequate and unconfident they felt. During my time with the refugees, I saw some real transformations. I saw the lightbulb come on for many of them. I continued to converse with many of them over several months, Skyping with them to find out how they were doing.

In Rwanda, I taught about the importance of identity as the first step toward enacting change. I presented an Identity Leadership workshop for top high school seniors. I also had the honor to meet with Rwandan president Paul Kagame, who has done so much to help Rwanda move toward self-sufficiency.

I have also traveled to China to conduct Identity Leadership workshops.

Every country I have visited, every group I have presented to, every connection I have made, I count as special. What I've learned from my travels over the world is that circumstances and cultures are different wherever you go, but people's needs are the same. And Identity Leadership workshops help build a strong foundation to meet those needs.

ENERGIZED TO SHARE THE PROCESS

I never get tired of teaching these nine steps, this identity leadership process. I love to see people's eyes light up in their aha moments of discovery, because I know where that discovery is going to lead them. I never thought that the process I was developing solely for myself would become so meaningful to people around the world. That is so gratifying. I consider it a tremendous privilege to share it now with you.

That's a glimpse into how it all began. That's my journey in this process. When you turn the page, you'll start your own identity leadership process. Prepare to be changed.

IDENTITY LEADERSHIP KEYS

- Many people assume the Nine-Step Success Process I came up with came easily to me, because the process itself flows smoothly and is strong and logical. It didn't. It was a painstaking process, one marked with stops and starts. But the journey was worth it.
- Along the way, I realized that you didn't have to be a global corporation or even a large company to be successful. You just needed a distinctive brand and a system that was built around a core that emphasized the strengths and purpose of the company.
- I also came to understand that such a system—built around a core of personal strengths and purpose—worked for

individuals as well. That was a real aha moment for me. The success process wasn't just a business thing. It was a life thing.

- The beauty of the nine steps is that they work at all levels, both for individuals and for organizations of all sizes. They are forged from life principles, with the key principle being identity. When the nine steps are effectively applied, they are not only powerful; they are life changing.

CHAPTER 9

Step 1:
Check Your ID

You are empowered when you know, define, create, shape,
and educate yourself so you can give of yourself.

In the last chapter I told you how the Nine-Step Success Process came about. It was a laborious process, but it was so worth it—as thousands of people around the world can attest. The beauty of this nine-step process is it works for anyone, anywhere, in any stage of life. It applies to the young, old, white collar, blue collar. It's a process, as I said earlier, that is geared to helping people self-actualize, reach their full potential, and fulfill their destiny.

So, you've heard about my journey in developing the nine steps. Now I want to prepare you for your own journey by describing in detail what each of these steps entails. In the next nine chapters I will briefly describe the step and provide some activations, which you can use to create your own identity leadership plan.

Do you remember those three questions I posed earlier: *Who are you? Where are you going? How are you going to get there?* The answers to those three questions are essential for you to understand. And before you begin a journey of any sort you need to know the answer to that first question, *Who are you?*

There is tremendous power in self-knowledge. Such knowledge seems simple on the surface, as if everyone automatically has a solid grasp on who they are, but as I've traveled the world and presented the nine steps and the identity leadership process, I've found that self-knowledge is a slippery and elusive topic, misunderstood or underemphasized by the majority of people with whom I've come in contact.

People assume they know who they are, but that assumption resides in knowledge that often doesn't delve far below the surface. True self-knowledge and self-understanding lie far beneath the surface, and it takes work to dig and discover who you are at your core. But it's worth the work because, just like an archaeologist during a dig, you can make some life-changing discoveries in the process.

Following are a few key facets of that dig that unearths the real you.

SHED LABELS, DEFINE YOURSELF

The first step to understanding your identity is to shun the labels that others have put on you, whether for good or bad. Any label, even a good one, is harmful if it is not an accurate description of your true self. You don't have to be a movie star or celebrity to have people fill your head with exalted images of yourself. That does you no good.

Most of the labels we get, though, are negative, demeaning, and limiting. They act as invisible clamps on us, throw water on the fire of our deep-down desires, and snuff out our potential before we even start.

To shun labels, we need to ignore people and listen to ourselves. We need the courage to dig down deep and discover and explore our true passions. We need to find out what makes us tick, what moves us, what inspires us, what energizes us, what brings us joy, and what brings out the best in us.

The ego is only an illusion, but a very influential one. Letting the ego-illusion become your identity can prevent you from knowing your true self. Ego, the false idea of believing that you are what you have or what you do, is a backwards way of assessing and living life.

—WAYNE DYER

MINE YOUR TALENTS AND DREAMS

Your identity is the intersection of your talents and dreams. It's the intersection of your abilities and your aspirations. It's the place where your gifts and your joys meet. That, at the core, is who you are, and knowing that opens the door to self-actualization.

That sounds deceivingly simple, but it's more complex than it seems. That's why so many people think they know their identity and have self-understanding when in reality they have only scratched the surface.

Why? Because either they don't really know what they're good at or what they deep down want to do, or because they *do* know but those talents and dreams have been squelched—by negative opinions of others, peer pressure, lack of resources, circumstances, or their own worldview.

Sometimes people are afraid to dream. They are afraid they won't achieve their dream, or they will look foolish, or they will risk too much in attempting to realize it. Sometimes it's the fear of failure, or the fear of success, or the fear of the unknown. I'll address these aspects in a later step, but for now, know that to achieve self-understanding it's imperative to know and explore your talents and dreams.

IDENTIFY YOUR CHARACTER STRENGTHS

Identifying your character strengths is a great way to deepen your self-knowledge. Understanding your strengths is the first step to being able to more effectively and efficiently use them and to build strategies—in your work life, your social life, all aspects of your life—to lean heavily on those strengths.

Self-awareness is the most important skill for career success.

—PETER GUBER

Create Your Value

At my seminars, I teach that the value you create for yourself is the value the world gives you. The world sees you as you see yourself. If the world doesn't see you for the value you know you have, then maybe it's how you're presenting yourself. Take a good, long look at that, and be honest with yourself. If you treat yourself with respect, the world will follow suit. If you value yourself, the world will value you.

It all hinges on love, which is the foundational piece for transformation. Self-love is a critical component of identity leadership. It all starts with self-love and builds from there. Self-love opens the door to self-leadership, and self-leadership opens the door to fulfilling your potential and realizing your dreams.

So, love yourself. Create your value. Live your dream.

CONSIDER YOUR WORLDVIEW

Your worldview is your philosophy of life—it is, as the word implies, how you see the world. A few common phrases related to worldview include "seeing the world through rose-colored glasses," being a "Pollyanna," or "seeing the glass as half empty."

Your worldview affects not only how you see the world, but how you see yourself. Worldview is more than just a viewpoint with a positive-to-negative spectrum. To give you an example of how worldview can affect you, if you fall on the negative end of that spectrum, you may hear an inner critic that is constantly saying "You can't do that!" "Don't be a fool!" "You're going to embarrass yourself!" "You aren't good enough for this!" "What do you think you're doing?"

This inner critic can convince you that you have far less potential than you actually do. It can con you into believing that your ceiling is low, that you should be happy enough where you are, and that you should not try for more. In doing so it can give you a false impression of yourself—one that inhibits you from achieving what you truly want to achieve.

WHAT MAKES YOU TICK

This first step, then, is all about understanding what makes you tick—your passions, hopes, dreams, and desires—as they intermingle with your talents, abilities, and experiences. It's about refusing to be labeled by others but rather letting the world know who you are. It's taking stock of your character strengths and seeing how those strengths can play out in various arenas of your life. And it's realizing how your worldview affects your self-understanding and has a great influence on your life.

This first step, then, is all about understanding what makes you tick—your passions, your hopes, your dreams, your desires—as they intermingle with your talents, your abilities, and your experiences. It's about refusing to be labeled by others but rather letting the world know who you are.

IDENTITY LEADERSHIP KEYS

- There is tremendous power in self-knowledge. Many people mistake self-knowledge as surface understanding, but it runs far deeper than that. It takes work to dig and discover who you are at your core.
- You won't be able to understand your core identity if you take on the labels that others put on you. Those people don't know the true you. Only you can know the true you—when you dig down deep to discover and explore your passions.
- Your identity is the intersection of your talents and dreams. It's the intersection of your abilities and your aspirations. It's the place where your gifts and your joys meet. That, at the core, is who you are, and knowing that opens the door to self-actualization.

CRAFTING YOUR IDENTITY LEADERSHIP PLAN

For each of the nine steps, you'll go through many activations that will help you answer the three questions that I have posed several times in this book: *Who are you? Where are you going? How are you going to get there?*

A word to the wise: *do not rush through these activations.* Give each activation and each question your full attention and focus. Don't do the activations when you're tired. There's no point in doing them if you don't have the energy and motivation to tend fully to them. These activations are meant to challenge you and help you dig deep within yourself. That's the path to self-discovery.

So, if you feel yourself flagging after you have gotten into an activation, stop. Come back to it later that day when you feel more energy or wait until the next day. The point is not how fast you can complete them. It's how well you can use them to create an actionable plan to self-actualize and reach your full potential in life.

That's why I call them *activations*: you are using them to activate your full potential.

Many times I will provide you with an opportunity to list five responses. List whatever is appropriate. It might be five, or it might be more, or fewer.

ACTIVATION 1: REALITY CHECK: WHO AM I?

Describe your **five best features or characteristics**. What do you like about yourself? Are you hardworking? Thoughtful? Loyal? Brave? Take your time and choose which features describe you at your best. (Others may or may not see these features in you as strongly as you do, for various reasons. But *you* know they define you at your best.)

1. _____

2. _____

3. _____

4. _____

5. _____

I am happiest when:

_____

_____

The fears that have most influenced my life are:

_____

_____

Three characteristics that might be holding me back from achieving more in life are:

1. _____

2. _____

3. _____

The biggest challenge or challenges in my life are:

_____

_____

_____

When I am faced with a challenge, my typical reaction is:

_____

_____

_____

ACTIVATION 2: DEFINING MY PASSIONS

List five or more things that you love to do:

1. _____

2. _____

3. _____

4. _____

5. _____

Now choose one activity from your list and answer the following questions:

My activity is:

_____

What I do now related to this activity:

_____

_____

_____

What I value about this activity:

_____

_____

_____

What I can do to increase my success in this activity:

_____

_____

_____

What more I want to accomplish in this area:

_____

_____

_____

ACTIVATION 3: RECOGNIZING MY TALENTS AND STRENGTHS

Sometimes people think *talents* and *strengths* are synonymous. They're related, but distinct. According to Gallup:[19]

> A strength is the ability to consistently provide near-perfect performance in a specific activity. Talents are naturally recurring patterns of thought, feeling, or behavior that can be productively applied. Talents, knowledge, and skills—along with the time spent (i.e., investment) practicing, developing your skills, and building your knowledge base—combine to create your strengths.

For example, if you enjoy meeting strangers and like making a connection with them, that's a talent. If you are able to consistently build and rally a network of supporters who are willing to help you, that's a strength.

Talents are innate and cannot be acquired; strengths can be developed.

My five best talents are:

1. _____

2. _____

3. _____

4. _____

5. _____

The talent that gives me the most joy or satisfaction is:

_____

My five best strengths are:

1. _____

2. _____

3. _____

4. _____

5. _____

The strength that gives me the most joy or satisfaction is:

_____

ACTIVATION 4: PUTTING IT ALL TOGETHER

You've considered your best attributes or characteristics, what makes you happy, what makes you fearful, what challenges you, and what holds you back. You've identified your passions, talents, and strengths.

Now take a moment to put all of that information together.

The five characteristics that define me best, which I listed in activation 1, make me capable in these areas or situations:

1. _____

2. _____

3. _____

4. _____

5. _____

Potential growth areas, based on my passions listed in activation 2, are:

1. _____

2. _____

3. _____

4. _____

5. _____

New outlets for my talents could be:

1. _____

2. _____

3. _____

4. _____

5. _____

My strengths might be better utilized in these areas:

1. _____

2. _____

3. _____

4. _____

5. _____

CHAPTER 10

Step 2:
Create Your Vision

Your life will evolve when you keep setting a higher vision for yourself.

S tep 1 explores that first question, *Who are you?* This step uncovers that second of the three questions, *Where are you going?* If you don't have a vision for your life, you're not going to know where you're going. You're just going to go where the currents of life take you, floating downstream not under your own power but under the power of the current. The fact that you are reading this book tells me that you want more out of life; you want to achieve things, test yourself, and stretch your boundaries and live a more fulfilling life than is afforded by just floating downstream.

CAST A VISION BASED ON SELF-UNDERSTANDING

With vision, you don't float; you pursue. Armed with the self-knowledge gained through step 1, you cast your vision based on your talents and dreams—based on your core identity. You begin to determine your future based on the potential that you can see through that self-understanding.

The very act of creating a vision for yourself brings an energy and purpose to your life. This is necessarily the second step because you cannot create a vision for yourself until you know yourself well. Vision follows understanding, and the greater the understanding, the clearer and more on target your vision can be.

Vision brings together two acts: the act of *being* and the act of *doing*. Because you know who you are (step 1), you can envision what you can do. Any potential roadblocks begin to melt away or crumble as you remain focused on both who you are and what your potential is.

Vision is really all about defining your journey. And it's a journey where you gain momentum as you move toward your vision. It's like a car trip to the Rocky Mountains. As you get into eastern Colorado, you can first glimpse a hazy rise in the far distance. As you continue on your journey, that hazy rise begins to become clearer and bigger. Soon you are seeing clearly defined mountains with jagged peaks and ridges. And your excitement builds as you draw nearer to your vision.

FUEL YOUR IMAGINATION

Vision fuels your imagination as you begin to map out your journey. Based on your skills and passions and other self-knowledge gained in step 1, brainstorm through various possibilities that appeal to you. Research options, talk to people who can help you further understand the options, and begin to create and hone your vision. It might be broad at first, but as you continue to pursue and investigate your options, it becomes more refined, more precise.

For example, based on your passions, interests, and abilities, perhaps you want to enter the medical field. You have the aptitude for science and related subjects, and you like the idea of helping people medically. But the medical field is very broad. It includes rehabilitation, diagnostic tests, dentistry, vision, hearing, healthcare, pharmaceuticals, nutrition, counseling, surgery, lab work, education, direct patient care, and much more. Based on your interests, you can knock out perhaps three-quarters of those choices, but three or four—perhaps nutrition, counseling, education, and direct patient care—stand out for you. So you research those disciplines, talk to people who are in them, take classes or otherwise educate yourself on them, and perhaps get an internship in one or more of them. As you proceed toward refining your vision, your choice becomes more and more obvious.

> *Vision without action is merely a dream. Action without vision*
> *just passes the time. Vision with action can change the world.*
>   —JOEL A. BARKER

SEE THE END BEFORE YOU BEGIN

That process I just described helps you to see the end before you begin. When you start a journey with the end in mind, you proceed with purpose and confidence. Vision gives you perspective because you can measure opportunities and experiences by how they align with your vision. If they will help you reach your vision, then you enter into those opportunities and experiences. If they will dissuade or distract you, then you veer away from them.

Vision gives you perspective because you can measure opportunities and experiences by how they align with your vision. If they will help you reach your vision, then you enter into those opportunities and experiences. If they will dissuade or distract you, then you veer away from them.

The Power of Vision

You have to have a vision bigger than yourself. Vision gets you beyond where you have been, beyond where you are now. It helps get rid of the historical baggage that some of us lug around. It helps you get beyond what you already know.

Einstein said you can't solve a problem with the same mindset that caused it. If you get stuck in that mindset, you can't evolve or grow. Vision helps you get beyond that mindset, get unstuck, and move onto a track of continuous improvement.

Knowing where you are headed gives you a reason to get up and get going each morning, because each day brings you one day closer to realizing your vision. You are motivated because you know that realizing that vision will allow you to reach your full potential and self-actualize. You are on your way to becoming the best version of yourself. You are headed toward your destiny and living the type of life you were meant to live.

You are headed toward a fulfilling and satisfying life, one in which your talents are in full use and your dreams are realized.

SET GOALS

To get to that place of fulfillment, you need to employ a key facet of vision-casting: setting goals.

Once you have created a vision for yourself, identify checkpoints along the way that keep you on track. In fact, let's use track as an example. Let's say two 1,600-meter runners have the same goal: to run a 1,600 in 5:00. Let's say Runner A is high on endurance but does not have any kick, any speed to rely on, at the end of her race. Runner B is so-so on endurance but has a blistering kick on the last lap.

Both runners have identified their own mini-goals, or check-points, along the way to help them run a 5:00 1,600. Runner A wants to run these splits for each 400: 72, 75, 75, 78. She figures she can get out faster because she has good endurance and can't rely on a strong kick at the end. Runner B's splits goals are 74, 77, 77, 72. She can't hold the same strong pace as Runner A, but she can run a much stronger last lap.

These are two runners with the same overall vision for their race and two different ways to achieve their vision.

That's how goals work: you figure out what's going to work the best for you to get you to your finish line. You don't set your goals based on how your peers with similar goals set theirs. You set yours based on your own strengths.

Here are a few things to keep in mind about goal setting:

1. **Goals should be realistic.** If you have no chance of reaching your goal, you're going to get discouraged and eventually give up. In that case, you will have failed at setting a challenging but realistic goal, not at reaching a reasonable goal. Set a goal that makes you work but that is achievable. You can always set higher goals once you achieve certain milestones.

2. **Goals should be meaningful.** Set goals that are directly tied to your vision. When you align goals with your vision, you are more motivated to work toward and reach those goals. Goals that don't get you closer to your vision can end up being distractions and time-wasters. I'm not saying you can't have goals that are outside of your vision—for example, you can have career goals and also personal fitness goals—but make sure you do have goals that tie into your vision.

3. **Goals should be well defined.** Vague goals such as "One day I want to start a business" are not useful. Research and think through the steps you will need to take to start your business,

and then create goals around those steps. A few examples of more specific, well-defined goals here are "I'm going to build my business plan by the end of October," "I'm going to meet with an insurance agent to talk over my business insurance needs in November," "I'm going to build my team within the next six months," and "I'm going to talk with and choose my vendors in December." These goals give you a direction to go in, a target to aim for, and a clear focus both in terms of what you need to do and when you want to do it by.

4. **Goals should excite you.** Let's face it, working toward goals is not easy. It takes a lot of concentrated effort, will bring on frustrations and challenges, and will try your patience. (And if goals don't do this, they are too easy.) So you better set goals that you're really motivated to reach, that excite you, that result in joy and satisfaction and a sense of accomplishment when you reach them. Otherwise, no matter how worthy the goals are, it will be easy to give up on them.

5. **Goals should follow a logical progression.** You likely will have many goals along the way to achieving your vision. Look at the big picture first, determining what you need to do to realize that vision, then break that down into manageable goals and see the relationship and the connection between the goals. They aren't independent of each other; they are linked together, like a chain, each link getting you one step closer to your vision. For example, in keeping with the idea of starting a business, let's say you identify seven goals: build your business plan, register with the government and IRS, purchase an insurance policy, build your team, choose your vendors, brand yourself and advertise, and grow your business. There is a logical, sequential flow to that order. But it wouldn't make sense to brand yourself and advertise first, before you even have a plan or a business that is in operation. Find the sequential

flow that makes sense and then go after each goal within that sequence. You can work on multiple goals at once—but you don't want to put the cart before the horse and work on goals that necessarily rely on other goals to be met first, if those other goals have yet to be met.

6. **Goals may need fine-tuning.** You've no doubt heard the saying "The best-laid plans of mice and men often go awry." It's a rare plan that never needs adjusting from start to finish. A critical skill in working toward goals is the ability to assess and adapt along the way. Don't be so tied to the original plan that you stubbornly forge ahead when it's wiser to see that the landscape has changed and your course of action should change with it. Here it is best to keep your focus on the overall vision—to see the forest for the trees, the big picture—rather than on the original goal, which is simply there to move you one step closer to that vision. At times you will have to take a sidestep or an alternate route to reach your vision. Be perceptive, assess your progress along the way, and be willing to adapt your goals as necessary to attain your vision.

7. **Goals should require positive action.** When goals are specific and measurable, you can more easily determine what practical steps you need to take to reach them. For example, "I want to lose some weight" is not a good fitness goal. "I'm going to run three miles tomorrow at 10 a.m." is a good goal. You know exactly what you need to do to reach the latter goal. Similarly, "I'm going to start eating better" is not a good goal. "I'm going to drink a protein smoothie five days a week and cut out fast food" is a good goal. Running three miles, drinking protein smoothies, cutting out fast food—those are easily measurable and require you to take specific action. By knowing what action you need to take, you know clearly whether you reached your goal or not.

Leadership is the capacity to translate vision into reality.
—WARREN BENNIS

The Nine Steps: Ever Relevant, Ever Dynamic

While there is a sequential order to the nine steps, I want you to understand one very important aspect of the steps. You activate each step one by one—that is, you engage it, get it going, experience it, and grow from it. But you don't then deactivate that step and move on to the next one. You activate them all, one by one, and you keep them activated.

These steps are meant to be fluid, variable, and open to change and transformation. For example, as you gain greater self-understanding and then move on to creating your vision, developing your travel plan, and continuing on with the other steps, you are going to learn things about yourself. You will likely reach new levels of self-knowledge, and with that new self-knowledge, your vision might expand or change, your travel plan might change, and other steps might change, too.

That's the power of the Nine-Step Success Process. It's not static; it's not "one-and-done" or "been there, done that." It's mobile, active, and dynamic. It has a flow and rhythm to it. If the steps were a body of water, they would not be a stagnant pond; they would be a flowing river, a sparkling body of water that is always moving, always changing.

And that means the nine-step process is valuable to you not just now, the first time through. It is valuable to you throughout your life. The principles undergirding the steps make the process freshly relevant to you today, tomorrow, next year, next decade, and as long as you have dreams, passions, goals, and aspirations.

IDENTITY LEADERSHIP KEYS

- Cast your vision based on your talents and dreams—your core identity. Begin to determine your future based on the potential that you can see through that self-understanding. The very act of creating a vision for yourself brings an energy and purpose to your life.

- Vision fuels your imagination as you begin to stake out your journey. Based on your skills, passions, and other self-knowledge gained in step 1, you brainstorm through various possibilities that appeal to you. It might be broad at first, but as you continue to pursue and investigate your options, it becomes more refined and precise.

- Goal setting is an important part of vision. Goals are the checkpoints along the way to realizing your vision. Make your goals realistic, meaningful, and well defined. Your goals should excite you and motivate you.

ACTIVATION 1: LIVING MEANINGFULLY

It's easy to get in the routine—or rut—of doing the same things day in, day out. We can float through our days without giving them much thought. But that's to our own detriment. To live meaningfully—to live intentionally, with purpose and the energy that comes with that intentionality and purpose—makes all the difference. So, think about the meaning and purpose in your life as you answer these questions:

What gives my life meaning? In what activities or pursuits do I find myself most energized?

_____

_____

Why does it give my life meaning?

_____

_____

_____

How can I enlarge the meaningful pursuits in my life?

_____

_____

_____

ACTIVATION 2: DARE TO DREAM

Forget money and any other obstacles for the moment. Sit back and dream a little. Don't put any limits on your dreams. Take some time to think through these questions: _In my dream job, what am I doing? If I could write my ticket, based on the talents, strengths, and passions that I identified in the previous step, how would I spend my work days?_

Again, take your time before you answer, because the first several thoughts that might pop into your head will come from learned expectations—from others and yourself. Dig deeper and free yourself to dream how you would fully utilize your talents, strengths, and passions. When you are ready, complete this thought:

In my dream job, I would . . .

_____

_____

_____

ACTIVATION 3: WRITING YOUR OBITUARY

This might sound morbid at first, but this is a great exercise to get you thinking about what you truly want to accomplish in life. I won't have you write an actual obituary, but I will have you answer questions that would lead to a revealing story of your life. How do you want to be remembered? What experiences do you want to have lived? Whose lives do you want to have touched? What do you want to have achieved? Thinking through these questions helps that bigger picture, that end goal, crystalize.

At the end of my life, I want people to remember me as this type of person:

_____

_____

_____

I want to live a life with these kinds of experiences:

_____

_____

_____

I want to have achieved:

_____

_____

_____

ACTIVATION 4: MY PERSONAL VISION STATEMENT

You've thought through what is truly meaningful to you. You've considered what your dream job would be. You've taken the long view of your life and visualized how you want to be remembered, what you want to have experienced and achieved. Now it's time to pull those ideas together and create your own vision statement.

A personal vision statement helps you clarify what is important to you. It acts as a rudder as you navigate through your days and helps you keep your focus on what matters amid everyday distractions.

As you think about your personal vision, keep in mind your values, your passions, your strengths, and the areas you want to grow in. Think about what energizes you and makes you happy. Think about how you operate best and your skills and abilities.

Make your vision statement short. You're not writing an essay; you're writing a concise statement that reveals your purpose, what is meaningful and important to you.

Here are a few vision statements from prominent businesspeople:

Joel Manby, CEO of Herschend Family Entertainment: *"I define personal success as being consistent to my own personal mission statement: to love God and love others."*

Richard Branson, founder of the Virgin Group: *"To have fun in my journey through life and learn from my mistakes."*

Amanda Steinberg, founder of DailyWorth.com: *"To use my gifts of intelligence, charisma, and serial optimism to cultivate the self-worth and net worth of women around the world."*

Did you notice how none of those statements talked about ascending to a certain position, attaining wealth or glory, or starting or expanding businesses? These statements are larger than that. They speak of how they want to treat others, the impact they want to leave on others, how they want to journey through this life, how they want to use their gifts to help others.

Now it's your turn. Take your time with this and come back to it over the next few days to refine it as necessary. Make it yours, make it meaningful, and make it inspiring—something that you can hang on to and that can guide you in your journey.

My vision statement:

_____

_____

_____

_____

CHAPTER 11

Step 3:
Develop Your Travel Plan

Having a purpose is what drives the action plan.

The third of the three big questions (the first two are *Who are you?* and *Where are you going?*) is *How are you going to get there?* That's what this third step is all about. In fact, steps 3 through 9 address that third question. But step 3 comes before the rest, because once you know who you are and where you want to go, you are best served by developing a plan that maps out how you can get from where you are now to your destination and achieving your vision.

Understand that the road to your vision is not all a clear, smooth, four-lane highway that you traverse in sunny and pleasant weather. In fact, the bigger your dream, the greater your obstacles will be along the way. You'll find yourself driving in fog, in sleet, in snow; you'll come upon traffic jams; you might blow a tire along the way or need other repairs. Maybe your planned-for road is under construction and you need to take an alternate route.

The point is to not get disheartened by the challenges and road-blocks along the way. Keep your focus on the end destination and figure out what you need to do to get there. And know that you're in good company when you experience setbacks and difficulties—because literally everyone who achieved anything of significance experienced setbacks and difficulties along the way.

Michael Jordan, who is always at the top of the list in any conversation about the best basketball player ever, was cut from his junior high basketball team. Maya Angelou, the remarkable poet, author, actor, director, and civil rights activist who received dozens of awards in her lifetime and more than fifty honorary degrees, was raped at the age of eight and was rendered unable to speak for several years because of the trauma. Franklin Delano Roosevelt, the thirty-second president of the United States, was permanently paralyzed from the waist down in 1921—twelve years before he became president.

We all have struggles and battles in reaching our vision. That's to be expected. And that's why developing a travel plan is so important, because it can help you overcome those struggles.

Here are a few suggestions for developing your plan.

TAKE ONE STEP AT A TIME

The excitement of detailing your vision and knowing where you want to go can give you great energy and momentum as you begin your journey. And that's good—you will need both energy and momentum all along the way. Just don't get too far ahead of yourself as you move forward. In your excitement, don't skip steps or try to look for shortcuts in your impatience to get farther down the road.

Remember that the journey is a process, one in which you learn along the way, develop your talents, and gain experience and understanding that will help you achieve your vision. Each step that you've outlined in your journey is important. Focus on the step, the place, and your current circumstances, and determine the action you need to take to complete that step and get to the next one. And understand that every step is not going to be glamorous or exciting, but each step is important in reaching your destination.

Remember that the journey is a process, one in which you learn along the way, develop your talents, and gain experience and understanding that will help you achieve your vision.

There are no shortcuts to success. Behind every gold medal performance by an Olympic athlete is thousands of hours of practice. The road to a gold medal is marked by hundreds if not thousands of checkpoints, like mile markers along a highway. To get to mile marker 145 you have to go past 141, 142, 143, and 144.

As you plot out your journey, it's important to remember that just as you are unique, so is your journey. Your vision and goals might not be unique, but your approach to them, your experience in pursuing them, will be uniquely your own. Learn from others who have gone down the path you are headed down, but don't try to match them step for step. Your talents, dreams, needs, experiences, and situation are all distinctly yours.

If you want to be happy, set a goal that commands your thoughts, liberates your energy and inspires your hopes.
—ANDREW CARNEGIE

PLAN AROUND YOUR STRENGTHS

You assessed your strengths in step 1; those strengths come into play now as you plan to use them to your fullest advantage in the pursuit of your vision or dream. Gallup has identified four domains of strengths, each with a number of themes: executing, influencing, relationship building, and strategic thinking.[20] (For examples of the themes, in the relationship-building domain, themes include developer, includer, harmony, empathy, and positivity, among others.)

The point is to understand what your strengths are—I will guide you in identifying those in the next chapter—and then focusing on them to move you ahead. If you are a relationship builder, you relate well to people, and you see how they fit into the bigger picture and interconnect with each other. You can bring groups together and help them to work more effectively as a team. Strategic thinkers are problem solvers and big-idea people. They are the vision casters, planners, and creative strategists.

So let's say your vision is to open your own restaurant. If you are a relationship builder, you focus on building a strong team, bringing together the right people with the right skill sets that will make your vision become reality. You bring in a partner or manager who has some of the strengths—including strategic thinking—that you don't have. If you are a strategic thinker, you cast the vision for your restaurant, you hire a manager who has the relationship-building skills that perhaps you don't, and you operate at both the bigger-picture level and the operational level, problem solving and strategizing to make the restaurant better and more successful.

The bottom line is that you focus on your own strengths and continually work them as you move toward your vision. You are at your strongest and best when you leverage your own talents. Home in on what makes you uniquely you—what you do best. When you consistently do what you do best, you will create a brand for yourself, become even better at your strengths, and move more rapidly toward your vision.

MANAGE YOUR TIME

When you manage your time well, you work more effectively, focus on your strengths more fully, and speed your journey toward your vision. According to a recent study by Salary.com, 89 percent of people admit to wasting time at work every day—with 31 percent wasting about thirty minutes a day and another 31 percent wasting an hour a day.[21] A survey by Harris Poll listed the top time-wasters for employees:[22]

- Personal calls or texts—50 percent
- Gossiping—42 percent
- Personal use of internet—39 percent
- Social media—38 percent
- Snack breaks, smoke breaks—27 percent
- Noisy coworkers—24 percent
- Meetings—23 percent
- Email—23 percent
- Coworker drop-bys—23 percent
- Coworker speakerphone calls—10 percent

When you have a bigger goal in mind you are more motivated to use your time well. But motivation does not necessarily equal execution. Here are my tips for managing time effectively:

1. Plan your time regularly.
2. Write weekly plans based on immediate goals. Review these plans daily and check off tasks you have accomplished.
3. Be realistic in how much you take on and in how much time you allot for each task.

4. Prioritize the most important tasks.

5. Don't take on more tasks unless you know you'll have time for them after you complete the tasks you must do.

6. Develop your concentration skills. Learn how to stay focused.

7. Eliminate self-distractions and focus on one thing at a time.

8. Set and keep deadlines.

9. Delegate tasks when appropriate and possible.

10. Encourage others not to waste your time. Learn how to close conversations when they're hampering your ability to get something done.

11. Slow down and regroup when you feel overwhelmed. Revisit your plans and prioritize your work.

12. Find time for yourself. Have some healthy outlets; this will help you manage stress and time.

Remember that pursuing a vision is a marathon, not a sprint. Pace yourself accordingly, move methodically forward, and look to use your time as efficiently as possible. You might be amazed at how much time you save when you put those twelve tips in action.

Our goals can only be reached through a vehicle of a plan, in which we must fervently believe, and upon which we must vigorously act. There is no other route to success.

—PABLO PICASSO

KNOW WHEN—AND WHEN NOT—TO STICK TO YOUR PLAN

There's a fine line between sticking to a plan too long and deserting one too soon. On one hand, you don't want to be stubborn or closed-minded when a plan is not working, or unaware that a plan needs revamping; on the other hand, you don't want to be impulsive and panicky, dumping or drastically changing a plan just because you fear it's not working exactly as you foresaw it.

Want an example of sticking to a plan? It's a humorous one, with me as the punchline, though it didn't seem so humorous at the time.

Many years back, Oprah and I were in Florida. I was a talented athlete—I had played pro basketball in Europe—and I had always enjoyed waterskiing. Oprah said she'd love to see me ski, so I was happy to oblige. I figured I'd show off some of that athletic prowess.

Well, that athletic prowess remained hidden as I tried, and failed, many times over to get up on the skis. (In my defense, I didn't have my custom-made slalom ski with me; the standard ones didn't fit my size 15 feet.)

I squeezed into that smaller ski and the boat would take off, and I would momentarily rise up on the ski, and then I would flop into the water. Not once, not twice, not three times, but *fifteen* times. The boat driver would look back sympathetically and say, "You want to go again?" I would nod, frustrated and determined, and Oprah said, "You better do whatever you can do to get him up on that ski, because he'll keep trying until he dies."

My body was taking a beating. My arms were swollen because of all the pounding by the water. To make a long (and painful) story a bit shorter, I didn't make it up that day. I was in a dark mood all that evening. I made everyone go back with me the next day. I was determined to ski until I got up or until my arms fell off, whichever came first.

Finally, on my twenty-third attempt (which made me think of the Twenty-Third Psalm—*Yea, though I walk through the valley of the shadow of death...*) I made it up. I was skiing. Everyone clapped, relieved—not least of all me.

Now, that was not a serious plan—but it was important to me in the moment. I stuck with it (and stuck with it, and stuck with it). I knew I was capable of it, and I was not going to quit until I accomplished what I had set out to do. Call that adventure "Persistence Personified."

Knowing when to stay with your plan and when to adjust it is more art than science. Sometimes you go with a gut feeling, especially if that feeling lingers for days or weeks. It's wise to get the advice of a mentor or a trusted objective observer if you're unsure. It's always good to have at least a few experienced confidants who can give you an outside perspective.

IDENTITY LEADERSHIP KEYS

- Once you know your identity and have a vision for your life or career, you need to have a plan in place to get to where you want to go. Expect to find obstacles along the way—but keep your focus on your destination and figure out, step by step, what you need to do to get there. And that will mean adjusting along the way.
- Your journey is a process, one in which you learn along the way. And your journey is unique to you. Even if you have the same vision and goals as other people, how your vision and goals play out is distinctly yours alone. Learn from others, but don't try to match them step for step.
- Because nothing goes exactly according to plan, you need to trust your instincts to know when to stick with your plan and when to adjust it.

ACTIVATION 1: SETTING GOALS

In the last two activations in step 2, you wrote about what you want to accomplish, what you want to be remembered for, what you want to experience, and what your personal vision is. With that in mind, write goals that will help you achieve what you want to achieve. I'm going to suggest a few different categories for you to focus on.

Write **SMART** goals—that is, make them **S**pecific, **M**easurable, **A**ttainable, **R**elevant, and **T**ime-based. (For example, a health goal might be to walk for at least thirty minutes three times a week for the next two months.)

My career goals:

1. _____

2. _____

3. _____

4. _____

5. _____

My personal goals:

1. _____

2. _____

3. _____

4. _____

5. _____

My overall life/legacy goals:

1. _____

2. _____

3. _____

4. _____

5. _____

Other categories of goals (name the category here, such as health, spiritual, etc.):

1. _____

2. _____

3. _____

4. _____

5. _____

ACTIVATION 2: ACTION STEPS TOWARD YOUR GOALS

Now take one of the goals you just wrote and write action steps for that goal—what you need to do to move toward and attain that goal.

For example, let's say your goal is to lose six pounds in six weeks. Some of the steps toward your goal might be:

- Go to bed by 10:30 p.m., because I tend to stay up late and eat junk food after 11 p.m.
- Walk at least thirty minutes five times a week.
- Cut out sweets—candy, ice cream, and pie. Instead, eat fruit or other healthy snacks.
- Use a nutrition app that tracks my nutrition so I am encouraged to eat more healthfully.
- Grocery shop when I am full.
- Cut my carbohydrate intake to 150 grams a day.
- Drink more water and cut out all sodas.

Now it's your turn. You can, of course, do this for more than one goal—in fact, I urge you to. But for now, focus on one to get you started.

My goal:

_____

My action steps toward my goal:

1. _____

2. _____

3. _____

4. _____

5. _____

ACTIVATION 3: STAYING FOCUSED

Go through the following list and rate each item based on how great of a hindrance it is for you in pulling your attention and motivation from following through on your goals. Then, in the lines below the list, write specific, actionable steps you can take to overcome any hindrance that you rate a 4 or a 5.

	1 No hindrance at all	2 A very rare hindrance	3 An occasional hindrance	4 A frequent hindrance	5 A consistent hindrance
Procrastination					
Stress					
Multitasking					
Technology/social media					
Coworkers/friends					
Boredom					
Wasting time					

Dwelling on the past					
Worrying about the future					
Dropping the important for the urgent					
Fear and anxiety					
Lack of purpose					
Apathy					
Lack of control					
Other _____					

My strategy for overcoming hindrances I rated a 4 or 5:

1. _____

2. _____

3. _____

4. _____

5. _____

CHAPTER 12

Step 4:
Master the Rules of the Road

You become what you focus on. Use your time wisely.

I magine how chaotic it would be if drivers had no rules to guide them on the road. The same goes for you as you move toward your own destination. In this section I'll share nine rules that I developed along the way in my own journey.

1. **Stay determined.** You will hit rough patches. You'll have plenty of opportunity to be discouraged and frustrated. Acknowledge the feelings and figure out a way to navigate through those rough patches. You won't get there if you give up after you hit a few potholes in the road.

2. **Listen to your inner voice.** That inner voice can tell you when things are going wrong, when you need to adjust, when you need to ask for help, and when you need to research something to help you on your way. It can guide you in making decisions. But do know that the inner voice can be a bit of a double-edged sword. If you tend to be pessimistic or have low

self-esteem, you might hear that inner voice telling you that you can't do it, that you're bound to fail. Learn to distinguish between a voice that comes from wisdom and one that emanates from fear.

3. **Unleash your imagination.** Imagination is directly tied to vision. The greater your ability to imagine, the greater the vision you can create. Imagination is about creativity, but it encompasses more than that. To use your imagination, it takes courage and the willingness to take risks. Imagination demands that you be open-minded, considering various angles and perspectives and possibilities. Imagination calls for you to see the extraordinary in the ordinary. One of the many benefits of using your imagination is it opens up many opportunities for you.

4. **Find balance in your life.** When you are working toward goals and are highly motivated to achieve, it can be easy to get out of balance—to have tunnel vision, to be a workaholic, to put all your eggs in one basket. This happens to the detriment of your relationships and your own physical, emotional, mental, and spiritual health. Yes, go after your goals. Just keep your goals and your life in perspective. A balanced life will help you reach your goals in healthier ways. You will recharge your mind and your spirit and come back to your goals refreshed and renewed. So, get regular exercise. Eat well. Get seven to eight hours of sleep each night. Invest in your relationships. Tend to your mental and emotional health. Just as you would seek help from a physician for a physical ailment, seek help from a counselor if you recognize you are mentally or emotionally unhealthy. Also tend to your spiritual well-being in ways that refresh and energize you.

5. **Be honest.** Be honest with yourself and with others. Trust is built on honesty. If people don't believe you, if they can't

trust what you are saying is accurate and true, you are going to be hampered in your relationships, which will impact your ability to achieve your vision. And when you are honest with yourself, when you recognize your limitations and issues you need help with and you seek advice or help, you will be better off.

6. **Do the work.** You can have the greatest plan in the world to achieve your vision, but if you don't execute that plan, it's not going to happen. Don't make the mistake of spreading yourself too thin and not giving each task the energy and focus it requires. And don't be a procrastinator. Martin Luther King Jr. said, "Faith is taking the first step even when you don't see the whole staircase." See the sidebar "10 Tips to End Procrastination" to help you here.

You can have the greatest plan in the world to achieve your vision, but if you don't execute that plan, it's not going to happen.

7. **Be positive.** Attitude is everything. Henry Ford said, "If you think you can do a thing or think you can't do a thing, you're right." A negative attitude sees closed doors and assumes they can't be opened. A positive attitude sees closed doors and assumes great opportunities lie beyond those doors, and goes to the doors to open them.

8. **Think things through.** Find the balance between seizing the day and responding judiciously. Yes, you want to move swiftly on good opportunities that come your way—but the key word there is *good*. Not everything that appears good at

first glance truly is. The investments, purchases, and decisions you make that will affect the progress on your vision deserve to be thought through before they are acted upon.

9. **See the big picture.** Identity leaders see the big picture—that is, they see beyond themselves. They see how their lives, enterprises, and vision can make a difference in the lives of others. As an identity leader, you are not creating opportunities for just yourself or working toward only your own vision; you are creating opportunities for others and helping them work toward their vision as well.

The only person you are destined to become is the person you decide to be.

—RALPH WALDO EMERSON

10 Tips to End Procrastination

1. **Write down your goal and give yourself a deadline.** These two simple acts can ignite action.

2. **Break your goal into small pieces.** Focus on what you can do today.

3. **Be accountable to someone.** Let others know about your goals and invite them to check on your progress.

4. **Stop thinking and start doing.** Sometimes we overthink things and get frozen. Doing some work—even if it's not well done and you end up redoing it later—is better than doing nothing. It gets you out of that frozen phase. Just take the first step.

5. **Make a decision. Any decision.** Theodore Roosevelt said, "In any moment of decision, the best thing you can do is

the right thing, the next best thing you can do is the wrong thing, and the worst thing you can do is nothing."

6. **Face your fears.** Don't make mountains out of molehills. Once you start working, those fears begin to diminish.

7. **Start with the hardest task of your day.** Even if—especially if—it seems humongous. You don't complete a marathon in a single step. You complete it in a series of steps, one step at a time. Focus on the step in front of you.

8. **Don't be a perfectionist.** Nothing is perfect—and something has to be done before it can be redone.

9. **Put your phone down.** Research shows that the average American adult spends between three and four hours on their smartphone every day. That time doubled from 2012 to 2018.

10. **Reward yourself.** Sometimes giving yourself a reward once you've finished a task or reached a milestone is incentive enough to move forward.

I can be changed by what happens to me. But I refuse to be reduced by it.

—MAYA ANGELOU

IDENTITY LEADERSHIP KEYS

■ As you move along on your identity leadership journey, several keys—I call them rules of the road—will help you. You need to expect rough patches and figure out ways around or through them. You also need to listen to your inner voice as you need to fine-tune or adjust your route. And you need to give your imagination free rein to create and to see possibilities.

- The journey is a long one. You need to find and maintain balance in your life—taking care of your mental, emotional, physical, and spiritual health.
- Identity leaders have the ability to see beyond themselves. They see the big picture and how they fit in. They see how they can make a difference in that big picture.

ACTIVATION 1: YOUR DEFINING CHARACTER TRAITS

From the following list, select two sets of up to five character traits. The first set will be composed of those traits you believe you excel in. The second set will include the traits that you believe are important to your leadership abilities but that you need to improve in.

Character Traits		
Accountable	Discerning	Nonjudgmental
Affectionate	Empathetic	Open-minded
Careful	Engaging	Optimistic
Charitable	Friendly	Principled
Committed	Generous	Reliable
Compassionate	Honest	Reasonable
Consistent	Humble	Responsible
Convicted	Imaginative	Humorous
Courageous	Kind	Sincere
Curious	Loyal	Uncompromising
Dependable	Modest	Unselfish
Diligent	Moral	Other(s):

Step 1: Choose the traits that best define you, the traits you excel in and that others would recognize as strengths in you. Choose up to five traits.

1. _____

2. _____

3. _____

4. _____

5. _____

Step 2: Choose the traits that you believe are important to your success as an identity leader but that you need to grow in. Choose up to five traits.

1. _____

2. _____

3. _____

4. _____

5. _____

ACTIVATION 2: YOUR OWN RULES OF THE ROAD

Go back to those ten traits from the previous activation—your five strengths plus the five in which you want to grow the most. Use those traits to draw up your own rules of the road.

Step 1: Think through how you can use those five strong traits to develop further as an identity leader. List each trait again and note how you can leverage that trait for further growth.

1. _____

2. _____

3. _____

4. _____

5. _____

Step 2: Think through what you can do to strengthen the five important traits that you feel you need growth in.

1. _____

2. _____

3. _____

4. _____

5. _____

CHAPTER 13

Step 5:
Step into the Outer Limits

Release the fear and move toward what can be.

*T*he *Outer Limits* was a science fiction TV show in the mid-1960s that was on the creepy side. It always began with a voiceover narration that told you not to attempt to adjust your TV picture; they were controlling it. They were controlling the volume, the horizontal, the vertical, the sharpness, and, by implication, you.

Stepping into the outer limits is scary for lots of people because doing so requires taking risks. And taking risks means you aren't in control of the outcome. You might fail. You might look silly or be humiliated (or both). Who wants to risk that?

Well, *you* do. Or at least you should. Let me explain why.

TAKING RISKS

I'm sure you've heard the saying "Nothing ventured, nothing gained." Imagine a butterfly that stayed forever in its cocoon. To emerge from the cocoon is a natural process in the life of the butterfly; to avoid it would literally kill the butterfly and deprive the world of seeing the beauty of the butterfly as it spread its wings and flew.

Now, playing it safe will not literally kill you, because you have a choice in the matter. You can choose to risk nothing in your life—but you pay a consequence in doing so. Listen to what these people have to say about taking risks:

- Mark Zuckerberg: "The biggest risk is not taking any risk. In a world that's changing really quickly, the only strategy that is guaranteed to fail is not taking risks."
- Frank Scully: "Why not go out on a limb? Isn't that where the fruit is?"
- William G. T. Shedd: "A ship in harbor is safe, but that is not what ships are built for."

If you want to achieve something you're reaching for, if you want to realize a dream that you have long held in your heart, you are going to have to put yourself out there to make that happen. And putting yourself out there means taking risks.

LEAVING YOUR COMFORT ZONE

You are the king or queen of your comfort zone. You reign over everything in it. You control everything in it. You know everything in it.

Yet, for many, their comfort zone is in reality more a prison than anything else, keeping them from experiencing all that life has for them. It's like one of those invisible fences that keeps dogs in their yard. They might see the wide world beyond, but they don't stray beyond their yard.

Again, dogs with invisible fences don't have choice—but we do.

We have the choice to go beyond our comfort zone. And do you

For many, their comfort zone is in reality more a prison
than anything else, keeping them from experiencing
all that life has for them. It's like one of those invisible
fences that keeps dogs in their yard. They might see
the wide world beyond, but they don't stray beyond
their yard.

know what will happen when we venture into our outer limits beyond
our comfort zone?

- We'll find challenge and struggle.
- We'll encounter fear and frustration.
- We'll experience failure—and success.
- We'll acquire new information and knowledge.
- We'll learn things about ourselves that we never could have
  learned any other way.
- We'll grow.
- We'll gain confidence and wisdom.
- We'll learn how to determine when to take a risk and when
  not to.
- We'll hone old skills and gain new ones.
- We'll meet people that will help us grow.
- We'll gain greater clarity of our vision.
- We'll stumble and fall.
- We'll get back up again.
- We will be tested along the way.
- We'll gain in strength and courage as we go through those tests.
- We'll be inspired to stretch even further.

- We'll realize the value of leaving our comfort zone and wish we had done it sooner.
- We will no longer fear failure.
- We'll find greater joy in our daily lives because we are doing what we were meant to do.
- We'll stop being controlled by what other people might think of us.
- We'll have more and greater opportunities open up to us.

My point is not that comfort zones are bad. Comfort zones are indicators of where our strengths are. We are comfortable in them because that's where we are strongest. So comfort zones are not bad at all.

My point is that we should want to *expand* our comfort zones. We should want to deepen the skills we have and learn new ones when those new ones are important to achieving our vision. We should take on new experiences that will help us move toward that vision.

It's really about extending those boundaries, extending your range, and giving you the freedom to move in the direction and toward the new experiences you need to be an identity leader.

As you move outside of your comfort zone, what was once the unknown and frightening becomes your new normal.

—ROBIN SHARMA

OVERCOMING FEAR

Fear is a powerful emotion, and it is often used in self-preservation. It warns you about dangerous situations: someone driving recklessly toward you, a gang of thugs approaching you on a dark street, your house catching on fire. Those are all fearful situations, and the emotions that arise help you respond to the situation at hand.

But fear is common in other circumstances as well, and being cowed by the emotion in these cases can actually harm you. For example, you don't apply for a new job, you don't take a certain class, you don't explore new skills or experiences, or you don't move to get on a team project because you fear you will be found deficient.

In these cases, fear can be crippling and hold you back from what you can and want to achieve. Identity leaders need to learn to not give in to these types of fear. When people look back on chances not taken and opportunities missed, fear is the common denominator. Their reasons for holding back might be different, but they all boil down to being fearful about what would happen if they tried something.

And so, sadly, they don't try anything. All they can do is look back at the end of their lives with regret that they didn't try.

Check out the sidebar "Seven Keys to Overcoming Fear" for some practical suggestions in doing just that.

Seven Keys to Overcoming Fear

Fear can be debilitating. But it can also be conquered. Here are some tips for how to do so.

1. **Define your fear.** Sometimes fears are vague and elusive—you're afraid, but you don't know why. You need to know your opponent before you can beat him. Are you afraid of public speaking? Of leading a team that has Person X on it? Of large-group meetings? Of working through an issue with an employee in your charge? Knowing your fear can place you in a position of power over it.

2. **Understand the root of your fear.** Next, dig down deep to understand *why* you have that fear. What is it about Person

X or large-group meetings that gives you sweaty palms or a feeling of dread? Why are those situations fearful?

3. **Visualize success.** Rather than fretting about your performance in a fearful area, see yourself performing calmly, confidently, and effectively. Visualization is a skill used by successful people in all walks of life, fields, and endeavors.

4. **Be proactive.** Overcoming fear is a battle. In battle, you can't fight when you are retreating. When you are reactive, you give the enemy—fear—the upper hand. When you are proactive, you put fear on the run. Being proactive means coming up with a plan—measurable, practical steps to overcome your fear.

5. **Step out of your comfort zone.** This is a necessity for you to face your fear, because your fear is never going to be found inside your comfort zone. So you will have to step out to meet it. That's where visualizing success will help you—it will give you the courage to step out.

6. **Face your fear—regularly.** No one truly wants to face their fear. But it's the most critical step to defeating it. Why? Because when we are repeatedly exposed to the same fearful stimulus, it becomes boring and mundane. On the other hand, if we avoid something we fear, it only grows bigger and scarier. For example, let's say you fear public speaking. If you avoid it, the fear just grows, and you panic if you are forced to talk in public. If, however, you seek out opportunities to speak—even short and informal talks—you find that they aren't so bad after all. That you can survive them. You might even come to enjoy them.

7. **Focus on the present.** One of fear's strengths is in worrying about the future. The future is unknown, and the

unknown can be scary. Fear wants you to keep looking at the future. What you need to do, however, is be aware of the present. Are you okay now? In terms of whatever your fear is, what is your reality in the moment? More than likely, it is good, or at least okay—nothing at all like the picture that fear is painting for your future. Focus on the truth of your well-being, not the potentially fearful things that might (or might not) happen in the future.

I learned that courage was not the absence of fear, but the triumph over it. The brave man is not he who does not feel afraid, but he who conquers that fear.

—NELSON MANDELA

IT'S OKAY TO FAIL

Everyone who has achieved anything of magnitude has experienced a lot of failure along the way. *Everyone.* Failure is the gateway to success.

Thomas Edison, on his way to inventing the lightbulb, said, "I have not failed. I've just found 10,000 ways that won't work."

Winston Churchill said, "Success is stumbling from failure to failure with no loss of enthusiasm."

J. M. Barrie said, "We are all failures—at least the best of us are."

C. S. Lewis said, "Failures are finger posts on the road to achievement."

These are all men who achieved greatness, and the common thread in their messages is that it's not only okay to fail; it's necessary if you are to achieve to your fullest potential.

Failure is temporary. And while it can be painful to experience, it is also a great teacher. We learn what we did wrong. We learn what we need to improve. We learn different tactics and strategies. We come upon new opportunities.

We learn many valuable lessons from failure—but perhaps the most valuable lesson is that it's okay to fail. Failure is neither permanent nor debilitating. It's not as bad as we thought it was, just as fear—when we face it—is not as bad as we thought it was. Failure is an experience we learn from, grow from, and move on from—all the better for the knowledge we've gained and actually one step closer to what we want to achieve.

Yes, failure can still move you closer to your goal. Because, to paraphrase Edison, you've found one more way that doesn't work. In knowing what doesn't work, you move ever closer to what *does* work.

But you don't move closer, if you don't risk failing.

IDENTITY LEADERSHIP KEYS

- To achieve something great, to reach your vision, you are going to need to take risks. You can't stay in your comfort zone, keep on doing what you have always done, and expect to grow and achieve what you haven't already achieved.
- Fear can be crippling in your identity leadership journey. Fear can hold you back from fulfilling the promise that is inherent in your gifts and abilities. You need to meet fear head-on, understand its roots, and be proactive in overcoming it.
- Many people don't take risks or leave their comfort zones because they are afraid to fail. Highly successful people fail—a lot—and they use those failures to learn and grow and get to where they otherwise could not. You can learn many valuable lessons from failure.

ACTIVATION 1: EXTENDING YOUR COMFORT ZONE

Answer the following questions to help you determine what your comfort zone is—and how you can push beyond it.

What is your comfort zone in your professional life? What are the upper limits of what you are comfortable with in your working world?

_____

_____

_____

What makes you uncomfortable about going beyond that zone?

_____

_____

_____

How does this comfort zone limit you?

_____

_____

_____

What professional growth lies beyond that comfort zone?

_____

_____

What holds you back from going beyond your comfort zone?

_____

_____

_____

What would motivate you to go beyond your comfort zone?

_____

_____

_____

What are three actions steps you can take to move beyond your comfort zone?

1. _____

2. _____

3. _____

ACTIVATION 2: TAKING RISKS TO TAKE FLIGHT

If you are unwilling to take risks, you're like an airline pilot who is grounded unless he or she does what is necessary to become airborne again. But being airborne affords you a great view of the lay of the land, helping you to expand your vision and reach your goals much quicker than if you remain on the ground. Answer the following questions to assess your risk-taking abilities.

What is the one risk you could take today that could move you more efficiently and effectively toward fulfilling your vision?

_____

_____

_____

What do you most fear about taking that risk?

_____

_____

_____

What is the worst thing that could happen if you took the risk and failed?

_____

_____

_____

What is the best thing that could happen if you took the risk and succeeded?

_____

_____

Would you survive if you took the risk and failed? Why?

_____

_____

What is the last significant risk you took, and what was the outcome?

_____

_____

_____

Why did you decide that risk was worth it?

_____

_____

_____

What did you learn from taking that risk?

_____

_____

_____

CHAPTER 14

Step 6:
Pilot the Seasons of Change

You have the power to change, and that is the challenge.

The nature of life is change. And while many people don't like change, you have to admit that life would be pretty boring if every day was the same. It would be like the movie *Groundhog Day*, in which Bill Murray was stuck in the same day for days on end. Being stuck in the same day every day would be a bigger nightmare than constantly facing change.

So the question becomes, how do we manage change? That's what we'll explore in this section.

WELCOMING CHANGE

I just said that most people don't really like change. This is the same as being reluctant to leave your comfort zone and being afraid to face your fears, which we talked about in the previous step. But the identity leaders who are moving forward the fastest and achieving the most are those who welcome change in their lives.

The identity leaders who are moving forward the
fastest and achieving the most are those who welcome
change in their lives.

It's a glass half full versus glass half empty outlook. When you
view change from an optimistic stance, everything—pardon the
pun—changes. Here's a comparison of a positive outlook of change
vs. a negative outlook:

Positive outlook	Negative outlook
Welcomes change	Fears change
Sees opportunity	Sees loss
Visualizes success	Visualizes failure
Is not afraid to fail	Fears failure
Is energized	Is anxious
Wants growth	Wants status quo
Is a leader	Is a follower

Every book and movie has turning points—plot points that are
pivotal events, often surprising events, that energize the story and
move it forward in unexpected ways as the story races to its conclu-
sion. That's exactly what change is for us. They are the plot points
in our life, moving us forward in often unexpected ways toward our
goals.

Yes, change can be packaged in a box labeled "contents unknown."
And depending on what's at stake, that box can be a bit scary to open.
But identity leaders are not afraid to open it. Do you know why?

Because they know one of two things will happen: the change will
be good and open up immediate new opportunities for growth and
leadership, or the change will bring with it challenges—which they

will turn into new opportunities for growth and leadership. That's not to say that all change is good or easy; it's to say that identity leaders know how to handle change, work through it, and ultimately make it good. They know how to deal with even difficult change.

In other words, identity leaders master the change, rather than letting the change master them.

When you view change from that angle, you come to welcome it, because you know it will ultimately be good.

Your life does not get better by chance, it gets better by change.
—JIM ROHN

NAVIGATING THE STAGES OF CHANGE

As I've studied change, I've identified four stages that we all experience with it. Here's a brief look at the stages of change.

Stage 1: Change Appears

In this stage, we need to let go of old things and welcome new things. Easier said than done, right? The old is known and comfortable; the new, even if exciting and promising, is still unknown and comes with challenges and risks. We don't like to let go of old things, particularly if we judge them as good, but sometimes even if we judge them as bad or less than desirable, we can find ourselves reluctant to give up what we have grown accustomed to. You often see this with women who are abused yet stay in the abusive relationship.

Stage 2: We Respond to Change

In stage 2, we respond to the coming change—sometimes negatively, sometimes positively. It's okay to have negative emotions about impending change. In fact, it's important to acknowledge whatever emotions you have. Change sometimes means letting go of the good to gain the better. In that case, we can find ourselves dealing with anger, sadness, anxiety, or a host of other emotions about letting go of what we already judged as good. Even good change can bring with it a sense of loss. Know that, deal with it, and prepare to move on to what's ahead.

Stage 3: We Engage with Change

In this stage, the change is fully upon us. It is no longer imminent or fast-approaching; we are immersed in it, for better or for worse.

Sometimes engaging with change can be like riding a bull. Sometimes you feel like you've got the hang of it, and then in the next moment, you're holding on for all you're worth.

As you engage with change, here are a few tips:

- **Move forward.** Don't get mired in looking back or longing for the good old days. Set your sights on the present and on what's ahead. This is the point where you need to embrace the change, because you need to be present in the reality you are in.
- **Be prepared to expand or shift your vision.** Your vision is not meant to be stagnant. It grows and develops as you grow and develop. Change is a time to revisit your vision and explore how it is affected by the change. Change often unveils new opportunities for growth, so look for those opportunities and adjust your vision accordingly.
- **Take it step by step.** This is equally true whether you are excited by the change or are dreading it. Either way, you can only take it a step at a time. Don't get caught up in wondering what it's going to be like six months or a year down the road.

Just focus on what you need to do and learn today. Tomorrow will take care of itself.

- **Stay focused on your primary goals.** Change has a way of rattling our cages. That's not all bad, but in doing so it can take our focus off our goals. Don't lose sight of your goals as you grapple with the change in your life.
- **Take care of yourself.** Change can be exhilarating…and exhausting. It takes a lot of energy out of us and demands a lot of attention from us. In the midst of change we can easily neglect our overall health—physical, mental, emotional, and spiritual. We can neglect our relationships and responsibilities that lie outside of the change zone. When you take care of your overall health and maintain healthy relationships, you position yourself to better manage change.

If you always do what you've always done, you'll always get what you've always got.

—HENRY FORD

Stage 4: We Grow through Change

This is the stage where it all pays off. We can and will grow through change—no matter how good or how bad it seems in the beginning—when we:

- Let go of the old things and embrace the new
- Acknowledge all our emotions regarding the change and manage them effectively
- Have a positive attitude toward change
- Move forward with change
- Stay focused on our goals
- Take care of ourselves through the process

Don't expect the growth to be one continuous smooth effort. It can be a two steps forward, one step back venture. It can be stop and start. It can appear to not be going anywhere, but when you look back, you may realize you were making slow progress all along.

Try journaling during this stage, and all the stages, of change. It can help you keep track of where you are not only in the moment but along the path of change. It can help you more easily detect the progress you've made, the new skills and experiences you've acquired, and the things you've learned. This can both reassure you and help you navigate the stages of change.

IDENTITY LEADERSHIP KEYS

- Identity leaders are not afraid of change—in fact, they learn to embrace it and use it to their advantage.
- Change necessitates letting go of the old and embracing the new. It brings with it a range of emotions and often a sense of loss, but when we engage with it, we can begin to see the new opportunities that it presents us.
- When we have a positive attitude toward change, we will experience growth through it.

ACTIVATION 1: LETTING GO

Sometimes change is hard because it means we have to let go of some things that we don't want to give up. Answer the following questions to help you sort through this issue.

Think of a change in your life that you reluctantly went through recently or are going through now. (I'll talk as though it is past, though it might still be in the present for you.) What were you required to give up during this change?

_____

_____

_____

Were any of these things difficult to give up? If so, why?

_____

_____

_____

How did you feel once you let go of them?

_____

_____

_____

What change happened once you let go of them?

_____

_____

_____

If you haven't yet fully let go of them, what would help you do so?

_____

_____

_____

If you don't fully let go of them, what will happen?

_____

_____

ACTIVATION 2: EMBRACING CHANGE

Embracing change can be difficult, even if we believe that it could eventually benefit us. Yet, to grow, we must experience and embrace change. Answer the following questions to help you gain a healthy perspective on embracing change.

When facing change that has an unknown outcome, my general attitude toward it is...

1. I run and hide.
2. I cautiously approach the change and poke it lightly to see if it is dangerous.
3. I approach the change with an open mind and explore its possibilities.
4. I run toward the change with open arms, embracing it with glee and exhilaration.

You've probably guessed that number 3 is the healthiest answer. The rest of the questions will help you explore why you respond to change as you do, and how you can adopt a healthy attitude toward it.

The reason I find it difficult to be open to exploring change is...

_____

_____

I can adopt a healthier mindset toward change by... (circle all that are appropriate)

1. Exploring all its possibilities
2. Seeing the possible benefits and opportunities that can come from it
3. Visualizing myself responding positively to the change
4. Considering the worst outcome and seeing that I will be all right even in that case
5. Taking these actions or thinking these thoughts:

_____

_____

_____

When I look back on significant changes in my life, I see that I... (circle all that are appropriate)

1. Weathered it
2. Grew from it
3. Adapted to it
4. Learned from it
5. Ultimately benefited from it
6. All of the above

Hopefully you can circle most of those numbers, if not number 6.

People or resources who can help me navigate change include...

_____

_____

My understanding of who I am as an identity leader can help me embrace change because...

_____

_____

_____

CHAPTER 15

Step 7:
Build Your Dream Team

Building a team is building strength.

N eil Armstrong walked on the moon in 1969. Michael Jordan won six NBA championships. Both are amazing accomplishments. Without taking anything away from either man, I do want to point out, however, that Armstrong would not have walked on the moon without the support of literally a cast of thousands from NASA, and Jordan would not be sporting six rings if he didn't have tremendously talented teammates contributing to those championships (including Scottie Pippen, who also won six rings).

There are also numerous amazing team achievements in which no one person stood out:

- **SEAL Team Six:** This is the team that took out America's public enemy number 1, Osama bin Laden, in 2011. The SEALs are the Navy's elite, and Team Six is the elite of the elite. (For one thing, they can swim hundreds of feet with their hands and feet bound.) They are also trained to withstand arctic temperatures and tear gas. They are tremendous examples of not only what the human body can do but what a team can achieve under the highest of stress.

- **Walt Disney and his team of animators:** Together they revolutionized children's films and created some of the most memorable characters in cartoon history—but not before multiple early failures. Disney and his fellow creators stuck to their vision and went on to make history.
- **The Google team:** Sergey Brin and Larry Page, founders of Google, originally did not see eye to eye. But they worked through their differences and created the most popular site on the internet. Google and its affiliated websites comprised about 63 percent of all core search queries in the US in late 2018.[23]

It takes a lot of people to accomplish great things. Americans like to glamorize the lone wolf and the icon who does everything on his own, but greater things can be accomplished by combining the strengths of many.

This holds true for whatever your vision is as well. In fact, I will go so far as to say that no one makes it alone. Building and maintaining mutually supportive relationships is essential if you are to achieve your goals in life. As a bonus, it makes going after your goals more enjoyable as well.

Putting together your dream team will help you realize your vision. So let's explore how to go about doing that.

PUTTING TOGETHER YOUR TEAM

Let's say you are a rising middle-distance track athlete with Olympic aspirations. While your success ultimately depends on you, chances of that success are enormously improved by the team surrounding you: coaches, trainers, physical therapists, massage therapists, sport psychologists, and sport nutritionists, not to mention sponsors who provide the funds to allow you to train. Then there are the fellow athletes you train with and another kind of team that offers financial and emotional support: family, friends, and significant others. To the vast majority of the world, when you step onto the track, it's all about you and how fast you can race. But you wouldn't be there were it not for your support team.

The same holds true in any field, discipline, or venture. The process is the same; it's just the setting that changes.

I want you to think about the type of team you need around you. That track athlete had all his bases covered: training, nutrition, massage, sport psychology. Every aspect of his training and performance was supported by one or more members of his team. You need to consider your own bases that you want to cover and the areas of help and support that are most important to you.

What are your weaknesses? Where do you need the most help? What do you need to learn? What do you need to be coached in and be evaluated and given feedback on? Where do you need to grow the most? What are your immediate challenges?

These are the types of questions to ask as you consider putting together an informal team of people to help you achieve your vision.

You can get what you want by helping others get what they want.
—ZIG ZIGLAR

FORGING POSITIVE PARTNERSHIPS

As you build your dream team, you will find yourself in at least two different types of relationships. One is where you currently are receiving more from the other person than you are giving. This typically occurs when you seek the advice of a mentor or advisor who is senior to you in both position and experience; they share from their experience,

Common Traits of Successful Teams

Whether you're part of a team that is informal or formal or that is composed of many people or just a few, here are five characteristics that successful teams share:

1. They are committed to a common goal.
2. They share common values and expectations.
3. They play complementary roles.
4. They have a plan for confronting and solving problems.
5. They have a plan for evaluating progress.

give you suggestions, and help from an objective viewpoint with little or no expectation of receiving anything of similar value in return.

Another type of relationship is on more of a peer-to-peer level, where you can learn from someone while also sharing your own experience and wisdom with that person.

In any relationship where you are gaining something that will help you develop as an identity leader, look to give back. In the case of a mentor or senior advisor, you likely won't be able to give back to that person (besides your gratitude), but you can look to pay it forward, helping someone as a mentor yourself one day.

HARNESSING TEAM POWER

The power of a team comes from bringing many people together who collectively have diverse skill sets that can achieve the team goal. Each person contributes his or her unique and necessary skills to the team effort. The idea is that there is strength in numbers—especially when you have the right skill sets and experience represented in those numbers.

When you have people around you who can give you diversity of thought, you can gain from that wisdom and experience and get further along than if you surround yourself with everyone who has your same level of experience and thinks like you. If everyone thought like you, you would know it all! And none of us knows it all. Gaining wisdom from diversity of thought will help you grow as an identity leader.

If everyone thought like you, you would know it all! And none of us knows it all. Gaining wisdom from diversity of thought will help you grow as an identity leader.

LEARNING FROM MENTORS

My experience with Bob Brown, an important mentor of mine who hired me in his company as vice president of business development, was invaluable. He gave me a solid foundation of knowledge in his public relations firm, which served Fortune 500 clients and other highly influential figures around the world.

Think through the types of people who can help you grow as an identity leader and achieve your vision. Then approach a few of them to see if they would be willing to meet with you occasionally to help you learn and grow in certain areas. Be specific about what you're looking for and why you are coming to them. The more specific you are in your requests, the better a mentor can determine if he or she can help you and the more productive your meetings will be.

Alone we can do so little; together we can do so much.
—HELEN KELLER

IDENTITY LEADERSHIP KEYS

- Having a team surrounding you and supporting you in your identity leadership journey is a critical aspect of achieving success. It takes a lot of people to achieve great things. No one makes it alone. So, look to build a dream team around you.
- In building your dream team, consider your weaknesses. Where do you need the most help? What do you need to learn? Who can teach you, coach you, and give you feedback and encouragement?
- Mentors can play important roles in your growth as an identity leader. Look to be mentored by someone who can help you in the areas where you most need help, and look for ways to give back to them as well.

ACTIVATION 1: ASSESSING WHERE YOU NEED HELP

A dream team consists of players with complementary talents and skills who work well together and know each other's strengths and weaknesses—and how the team can capitalize on those strengths while minimizing those weaknesses. Such a team calls for each player to know his own strengths and weaknesses and know when he should take the lead and when he should call for help. Work through the following questions to help you assess the areas you need help in, and when you should seek that help.

In terms of working toward and reaching goals, in what areas or aspects do you think you could use support or help?

_____

_____

Who are the most likely candidates who could help you in these areas?

_____

_____

_____

How would you approach this person or these people? What would you say to them?

_____

_____

_____

What type of arrangement would be most beneficial to both sides?

_____

_____

_____

ACTIVATION 2: TEAMING UP

In the previous activation you focused on specific areas or issues that you could use help on. In this activation you will focus more on helpful relationships and general guidance. With that in mind, think of five people you can contact who can act as mentors or otherwise provide wisdom and a good sounding board for you. These people should have your best interests in mind, ask probing questions that help you sort through issues, and offer honest and constructive criticism.

Five people who could act as mentors or sounding boards for me are:

1. _____

2. _____

3. _____

4. _____

5. _____

The best teams are those in which teammates help each other. So, for each of those five people, think through how you can offer them help.

I can help each of those five named above by:

1. _____

2. _____

3. _____

4. _____

5. _____

CHAPTER 16

Step 8:
Win by a Decision

*Once you decide who you want to be, you then have to
decide what you have to do to make that happen.*

You can have a firm grip on your identity, the best game plan for
your life, the clearest and strongest vision for what you want to
accomplish, and the wisest goals in place—but if you have trouble
making decisions, you are going to struggle to reach your full potential.

Sometimes people have difficulty with decisions for reasons I
have pointed out earlier: they have a fear of failure or a fear of the
unknown. Some drag their feet making decisions because it exposes
them to criticism and evaluation.

Making decisions is not an option in our lives. Did you know that
scientists have determined that an adult makes, on average, about
35,000 decisions a day? We decide what to eat, what to wear, where to
go, how to get there, what we believe, what we read and watch, what
we say, how we say it, how we spend our free time, and on and on.

Every decision has a consequence, large or small. But don't be
fooled: even the small consequences can add up to have a cumulative

effect. For example, let's say you make some poor nutrition and health choices today. No big deal. But let's say those choices become habits, and every day you eat poorly and don't get enough exercise or sleep. After a while, those little decisions add up to a big consequence, likely in the name of serious health problems and reduced quality of life.

Let's look at a couple of aspects of decision making: types of decision makers and the decision-making process.

TYPES OF DECISION MAKERS

People use a number of approaches when making decisions. Various factors influence the approach, including the situation, the potential consequences, and the personality of the decision maker. Let's look at some of those approaches here. Try to identify which type or types of decision maker you are based on these definitions.

The Emotional Decision Maker

You are impulsive, hasty, and rash in making decisions. You fly by the seat of your pants and go with what pops in your head or what moves you the most. One day you might decide one thing; the next day you might decide the opposite thing. Decisions are like hot potatoes: you get rid of them quickly.

If you are this type of a decision maker, you need to take a few steps back, take some breaths, think through some issues concerning a decision, and perhaps consult some people who should be in on the process with you. The old saying "haste makes waste" applies here. Reject the impulse to decide immediately based on your emotions and slow the process down.

Life is a matter of choices, and every choice you make makes you.
—JOHN C. MAXWELL

The People Pleaser

You spend your energy trying to figure out what other people want you to do or think. You tend to go with what you think will make others—particularly those who will be affected by your decision—happiest, either with you or the situation.

People pleasers often would decide a different way if left on their own, but they are too caught up in trying to please others. If you are like this, realize that even if people don't agree with your opinion or decision, they will respect you if you are honest and if you are convinced that you are making the right choice for the group.

The Delegator

You give others the responsibility to decide. There are many times, of course, where this is the appropriate route to take, and there can be times as well where you are just shirking responsibility for one reason or another. Delegating can help projects move along faster and help others grow in responsibility and leadership. It can also free you up to make more important decisions or to do other important work. On the other hand, make sure you are not delegating simply to avoid making a difficult decision that is rightfully yours to make.

The Denier

You ignore decisions because they seem too difficult or huge. You pretend they're not there. But ignoring a decision is a decision itself, and it usually makes the consequences worse. If you are a denier, work to get at the root of why you don't like to make difficult decisions or why you procrastinate.

The Balancer

You weigh decisions, considering all the factors involved. You think through all the options and consequences and arrive at your decision after going through this process.

If you are a balancer, you are in a good place as an identity leader and have highly developed decision-making skills.

The Prioritizing Decision Maker

Prioritizing decision makers tend to be leaders who have a lot on their plate. They prioritize their decisions based on which are most important to make now. They see the big picture and focus on what's important at the moment.

If you are a decision maker who likes to prioritize decisions, you have the type of decision-making skills and tendencies that you need as an identity leader. There is a big difference between prioritizing and procrastinating. Those who prioritize put off certain decisions for valid reasons and tend to the more important decisions first.

> *Sometimes it's the smallest decisions that can change your life forever.*
>
> —KERI RUSSELL

THE DECISION-MAKING PROCESS

Here are some strategies that can help you in the decision-making process.

1. **Weigh the issue.** What are the risks if you do change? What are the risks if you *don't* change? What is behind the change?

What stakes are involved? What are the pros and cons of potential decisions?

2. **Consider possible actions.** Think through various options. At times it might be simply a yes or no decision; at other times it might be a decision that has multiple options. Clarify what your options are and what your routes or actions would be for each option.

3. **Think through the consequences.** Next, consider the consequences of every option that you have identified. What can happen, both good and bad, if you take option A? Option B? Option C? What can you live with, and what can you not live with? What gets your closer to your vision?

4. **Take action.** Finally, decide on what you believe is the best route for you—and commit to it. That doesn't mean you commit blindly and follow that route to its bitter end, regardless of what you encounter along the way. But you do need to commit to fully investigating that route and seeing how your decision is panning out. If it is not panning out as you had hoped, and it is holding you back from your goals or vision, then you have another decision to make: do you take an alternate route?

As you know, life is full of decisions. Figure out what kind of a decision maker you are and look to weigh and prioritize important decisions and delegate lesser decisions when appropriate. And take your time through the decision-making process, as outlined above. It's a critical part of your ability to grow as an identity leader.

Take your time through the decision-making process... It's a critical part of your ability to grow as an identity leader.

IDENTITY LEADERSHIP KEYS

- The decisions you make along the way, both big and small, impact your identity leadership journey. Be mindful of the decisions you make and weigh them against your overall goals and vision.

- Some people tend to avoid making decisions, perhaps fearing failure or because they are people pleasers, or the decision just seems too big. If you are one of these people, you need to get at the root of why it's difficult to make decisions and take steps to overcome those challenges.

- Part of overcoming the challenge of making decisions is to systematically go through the decision-making process. Weigh the issue, consider possible actions, think through the consequences of those actions, and take the action you deem right and best.

ACTIVATION 1: YOU MAKE THE CALL

Think of a decision that you are going to have to make soon or imagine a hypothetical but realistic decision you could face one day. Then answer these questions.

What is the decision you have to make?

_____

_____

_____

What are the pros?

_____

_____

What are the cons?

_____

_____

_____

How can this decision impact your career or your life?

_____

_____

_____

What is the worst-case scenario?

_____

_____

_____

What is the best-case scenario?

_____

_____

_____

Based on your previous answers—going by gut reaction—what do you decide you should do?

_____

_____

Why did you decide this?

_____

_____

_____

ACTIVATION 2: LOOKING BACK TO LOOK FORWARD

Sometimes seeing things in retrospect gives us the perspective to make wise decisions. Think through a past decision you have made to help you in a current situation.

What was a difficult decision you made that had a positive outcome?

_____

_____

_____

What made that decision difficult?

_____

_____

_____

Why did you decide the way you did?

_____

_____

What did you learn from that decision-making process that you can apply to current or future decisions?

_____

_____

_____

CHAPTER 17

Step 9:
Commit to Your Vision

What you spend your time on determines where you will go, what you will do, and how you will do it.

An essential ingredient in your journey to fulfilling your potential is your ability to commit to your vision. You need commitment because you *will* come up against roadblocks, failures, and disappointments. That's the nature of the game. And the people who win the game are the ones who stay committed, persevere, and maintain the discipline they need to come out on top.

Let me give you a brief example from my own life. As I mentioned earlier, I worked in the federal prison system—first in Denver, from 1980 to 1983, then in Chicago, from 1983 to 1986. When I was transferred to Chicago, I was placed in R&D—which unfortunately does not stand for Research and Development, but for Receiving and Discharge. In R&D, we had to conduct strip searches of all prisoners, both coming and going. It was embarrassing for me and for them. And this was a continual part of my job.

I can guarantee you, no guard likes doing strip searches. I was quickly asking myself, *How do I get out of this? How do I move to a better position?* Most of the guards complained about that aspect of the job, and I couldn't blame them. But I noticed that all the guards who complained remained in the same job. Their supervisor was in no rush to move them out. Sometimes, the more you hate your job, the longer it seems you have to stay in it. If all your boss hears from you is complaining, he or she is not inclined to help you move on to a better position.

So I decided to have a great attitude about my work—even the parts that I didn't like. I started talking about how great the job was, and whenever my boss would ask me how I was doing, I would smile and respond that I was doing great.

My attitude resulted in me becoming president of the employees club, where I worked to make things better for employees. I contributed to the employee newsletter as well. And one day, the warden came down and said, "We have an opening for a supervisor in the education department, and I understand you have a master's degree in education. Would you be interested in the job?"

I had to hold myself back from hugging the man. But I simply smiled and said, "Yes, I would be very interested."

My immediate vision, at the prison, was simply to get a better job. I had committed myself to being such a positive and dedicated employee that my bosses would have no choice but to promote me. If I had not stayed committed to my vision, that promotion would not have happened. If I had groused about my situation and did the minimum required of me, no one would have thought to place me in a higher position. My commitment to my vision not only helped me get through the drudgery of my current situation, but it propelled me to a better situation.

Commitment leads to action. Action brings your dream closer.
—MARCIA WIEDER

BELIEVING IN YOURSELF

It's hard to commit to your vision if you don't believe in yourself. It's easy to sail toward your vision on a sunny day in calm waters, but when those waters get choppy and a storm comes up, you have to believe in your navigational skills to see you through to your destination. Otherwise, you'll sink or veer far off course.

It's when those waters get rough that you have to dig down deep into the core of your identity, reaffirming who you are, what your strengths and passions are, what your purpose is, and what your vision is. When you know yourself and you believe in yourself and in your vision, that gives you the motivation to persevere through those choppy waters.

Think for a moment about David from the Bible. No one in the Israelite camp dared to go up against the massive giant Goliath; he would rip them to shreds and eat them for breakfast. But David—a young, lowly shepherd who was small in stature—said he would conquer Goliath. The Israelites tried to talk him out of it, but he had a very different vision, one that gave him the courage to step up and challenge the giant. And he did defeat Goliath, much to everyone's surprise.

David didn't shrink back in fear at the immense challenge facing him. He rose to the occasion, steadied by his vision, and he overcame the challenge. He believed in himself and in his vision.

When you have that same type of belief and commitment, you will be victorious, too.

COMMITTING TO SELF-ACTUALIZATION

Committing to your vision is really committing to self-actualization. It's saying, *Nothing is going to stop me from being the best I can be. Nothing is going to stop me from achieving my full potential. I'm going to unpack all that I have, I'm going to explore and deepen all of my abilities and strengths, and I'm going to pour all of those strengths and abilities into my passions and the pursuits that I was created for.*

Committing to your vision is really committing to self-actualization. It's saying, *Nothing is going to stop me from being the best I can be. Nothing is going to stop me from achieving my full potential.*

As I mentioned in chapter 7, self-actualization is your greatest need. When you self-actualize, everything else falls into place. The people who are the most successful people in the world are those who are self-actualized human beings. They're grooving away on all cylinders because they've got it all figured out. They are confident in themselves because they know themselves. They don't rely on other people's opinions of them, and they aren't dismayed if other people don't agree with them or have the highest opinion of them.

Why? Because as self-actualized identity leaders, they are too focused on living the dream—only for them, it's *not* a dream. For them, it's reality. For them, you can exchange *dream* with *passion* and *purpose* and *vision*.

Most people fail not because of a lack of desire but because of a lack of commitment.

—VINCE LOMBARDI

WHAT IT MEANS TO BE COMMITTED

Commitment is all about *doing*; it's not about planning, saying, writing, or hypothesizing. Commitment requires not just resolve, but *action*, such as coming to the fork in the road and turning down the rougher road because you know that's the road that leads to your vision. Commitment is about that rubber hitting the road, about you taking the action you need to achieve your vision regardless of the road or weather conditions.

Commitment is persevering and continuing to pursue your vision in spite of distractions, hardships, criticism, and risk. It is doing something because you believe it is right for you to do it. Why is this so important? Because the commitments you choose to make and fulfill in your life ultimately shape your life.

You can make a lot of mistakes on the journey to a fulfilling life without seriously harming your ability to achieve your dream. But it will not happen if you make the mistake of failing to fully commit to your vision.

On the other hand, great things can happen when you remain committed. Not easy things, not simple things. But great things.

Readjust plans as necessary. But never give up on your vision.

IDENTITY LEADERSHIP KEYS

- A vision is good only as long as you commit to it. That commitment takes a strong belief in yourself, your abilities, and your goals.
- Committing to your vision really means you are committing to self-actualization—the achieving of your full potential.
- Commitment requires action. You show your commitment by doing, not by planning. Yes, planning and setting goals and enacting all the other steps does take commitment—but the fruit of commitment is shown in your action, the execution of

your plan, and your continued pursuit of your vision, regardless of obstacles.

ACTIVATION 1: FINDING THE RESOLVE WITHIN

Sometimes keeping a commitment is easier said than done. This activation will help you explore some of the issues surrounding commitment.

An example of when I was unable to keep a commitment is...

_____

_____

I had difficulty keeping that commitment because...

_____

_____

I could have kept that commitment if I had...

_____

_____

In general, my biggest challenges in keeping commitments are...

_____

_____

When I am challenged to keep a commitment, this is what I can do to keep it:

_____

_____

_____

ACTIVATION 2: COMMITTING TO BEING AN IDENTITY LEADER

Answer these questions to help you firm up your commitment to be an identity leader and self-actualize.

My vision statement is: (revisit and copy over your vision statement from activation 4 in step 2)

_____

_____

_____

My most important goals in reaching that vision are:

_____

_____

_____

I am committing to this vision because...

_____

_____

I am able to stay committed to this vision because of these personal characteristics:

_____

_____

_____

CHAPTER 18

Become an Identity Leader

The world needs identity leaders. It will always need identity leaders—self-actualizing people who know themselves and can lead others in meaningful pursuits. Identity leaders will always rise to the top and stand out in a crowd, simply because they know the answers to the three crucial questions I posed early on in this book:

Who am I?

Where am I going?

How am I going to get there?

The vast majority of people can't answer those questions. When you can, you are an identity leader, and your talents and vision are going to be noticed. You will shine wherever you are, and you will rise to the position and place where you best fit in terms of your abilities, passion, and purpose. You will make valuable contributions to people's lives wherever you go—in work settings, social milieus, community and church organizations, whatever the situation might be.

The cream rises to the top, and identity leaders are the cream.

Identity leaders are buoyant. Where others sink, they stay afloat. Circumstances might delay them but won't stop them. They rise to every challenge they meet. They keep their heads about them in stressful and difficult times. They think clearly; they don't panic or make rash decisions. They stay the course that will get them to their destination.

Identity leaders see the talent, the gold, in others. And far from being threatened by that talent, they pull it out of others and help them develop that talent. They get the same type of joy in developing others that they do in developing themselves.

Identity leaders are in it for the long haul. They know that life is a journey to be both treasured and explored every step of the way. They know the great pleasure of mining their own gold as they travel along their path. They see the big picture and their final destination, but they are mindful of the surrounding scenery along the way.

Identity leaders know that the way to make the most of their life is to make the most of their twenty-four hours today, and to live each day with purpose. And that purpose is driven by their identity and guided by their ability to lead first themselves and then others.

Identity leaders are focused on their passion and vision. They are up to whatever task is required to live out their passion and realize their vision. They find the energy to keep going because passion and vision provide that energy.

Identity leaders are rare commodities—yet anyone can become an identity leader.

You just need to know the answers to these three questions:

Who am I?

Where am I going?

How am I going to get there?

To be an identity leader, you don't need a certain level of education, a certain IQ score, or a certain set of experiences. You just need the drive, desire, and dedication to learn the answers to those three questions.

It's as simple—and as hard—as that.

A FINAL WORD

The plan you have just created is an *action* plan—meaning you need to act on it to bring it to fruition. You have finished this book, but you have just started your journey as an identity leader. The activations you have worked through will be meaningful only if you make them so—if you live them out, act on them, and use them as tools to step more fully into your destiny as an identity leader. Return to this plan on a regular (at least annual) basis to see how you've grown and adapt it as necessary.

You are well on your way to furthering your potential as an identity leader. Keep on going! It's a journey that, no matter how hard at times, is well worth it. It's a journey that leads to the satisfying and fulfilling life that you have deep down envisioned for yourself.

My best wishes to you as you continue your journey.

Acknowledgments

I would like to thank Jan Miller for all of her support over the years as my agent. And I want to thank my co-writer, Tom Hanlon, for his support of, and dedication to, my work. It's always a pleasure working with Tom.

Notes

1. Constanza Montana, "Determined Mother of 8 Helps Her Kids Beat the Odds," *Chicago Tribune*, July 18, 1990. https://www.chicagotribune.com/news/ct-xpm-1990-07-18-9002280593-story.html.
2. Marc Cooper, "How Self-Awareness Impacts Leadership Success," Dental Practice Management, July 19. 2016. http://practicemanagement.dentalproductsreport.com/article/how-self-awareness-impacts-leadership-success.
3. "Creative Self-Leadership," Creativity Squads. http://creativitysquads.com/creative-self-leadership.
4. Ben Linders, "Self Leadership for Agility," InfoQ, February 2, 2016. https://www.infoq.com/articles/self-leadership-agility.
5. Ken Blanchard Companies, "Self Leadership." https://www.kenblanchard.com/get-attachment/Products-Services/Situational-Self-Leadership/Self-Leadership-Overview.pdf.
6. William Deresiewicz, "Solitude and Leadership," American Scholar, March 1, 2010. https://theamericanscholar.org/solitude-and-leadership/#.XC9fZy2ZN0I.
7. "Gallup-Purdue Index Report 2014," Gallup. https://news.gallup.com/reports/197141/4.aspx.
8. Susan Sorenson and Keri Garman, "How to Tackle U.S. Employees' Stagnating Engagement," Gallup, June 11, 2013. https://news.gallup.com/businessjournal/162953/tackle-employees-stagnating-engagement.aspx.
9. Jeff Schwartz, Bill Pelster, and Josh Bersin, "Human Capital Trends 2014 Survey: Top 10 Findings," Deloitte, March 7, 2014. https://www2.deloitte.com/insights/us/en/focus/human-capital-trends/2014/human-capital-trends-2014-survey-top-10-findings.html.

10. Richard Best, "John Rogers' story: Net Worth, Education & Quotes." investopedia.com.

11. Robert Chen, "EMBA Student Robert Chen, WG'19, an Executive Coach at Exec|Comm in New York City, Highlights Takeaways about Leadership from Mary Barra, CEO of GM," Wharton School, April 9, 2018. https://www.wharton.upenn.edu/story/8-insights-leadership-gm-ceo-mary-barra-wharton-people-analytics-conference.

12. Jim Souhan, "Vikings' chief operating officer knows no limits." startribune.com.

13. "What Makes a Great Leader? Daniel Goleman Answers," Leaders League, April 6, 2015. https://www.leadersleague.com/en/news/what-makes-a-great-leader-daniel-goleman-answers-truly-effective-leaders-are-distinguished-by-a-high-degree-of-emotional-intelli.

14. Kendra Cherry, "Left Brain vs. Right Brain Dominance: The Surprising Truth," Very Well Mind, September 21, 2018. https://www.verywellmind.com/left-brain-vs-right-brain-2795005.

15. Abraham Maslow, "A Theory of Human Motivation," Classics in the History of Psychology, August 2000. https://psychclassics.yorku.ca/Maslow/motivation.htm.

16. Abraham Maslow, "A Theory of Human Motivation," Classics in the History of Psychology, August 2000. https://psychclassics.yorku.ca/Maslow/motivation.htm.

17. David Sze, "Maslow: The 12 Characteristics of a Self-Actualized Person," Huffington Post, July 21, 2015. https://www.huffpost.com/entry/maslow-the-12-characteris_b_7836836.

18. Edward Hoffman, "The Life and Legacy of Abraham Maslow," Psychology Today, September 4, 2011. https://www.psychologytoday.com/us/blog/the-peak-experience/201109/the-life-and-legacy-abraham-maslow.

19. "What Is the Difference between a Talent and a Strength?" Clifton-Strengths for Students, https://www.strengthsquest.com/help/general/143096/difference-talent-strength.aspx.

20. Nathan Freeburg, "How to Understand the Four Domains of Strength," Deloitte, June 27, 2014. https://www.leadershipvisionconsulting.com/how-to-understand-the-four-domains-of-strength.

21. "Why and How Your Employees Are Wasting Time at Work?" Salary.com, April 17, 2018. https://www.salary.com/articles/why-how-your-employees-are-wasting-time-at-work.

22. Peter Economy. "The Top 10 Ways Your Employees Waste Time at Work," Inc.com, August 20, 2015. https://www.inc.com/peter-economy/top-10 -time-wasters-at-work.html.

23. "Share of Search Queries Handled by Leading US Search Engine Providers as of October 2018." Statista. https://www.statista.com/statistics/267161/ market-share-of-search-engines-in-the-united-states.

Index

About the Author

Stedman Graham has built a strong reputation for helping corporations, organizations, and individuals succeed. His life's work has been and continues to be focused on teaching the value and process of identity leadership. He is the author of eleven books, including two *New York Times* bestsellers, and is the chairman and CEO of S. Graham & Associates, a management and marketing consulting firm. He lives in Chicago, Illinois.